Finding My Shine

Finding My Shine

NASTIA LIUKIN

ISBN-13: 9780692561010
ISBN-10: 0692561013

Dedication

To all the girls out there with big dreams: Think bigger, work harder, and believe stronger, because dreams do come true. May you always *shine* in whatever you do.

Acknowledgements

To my amazing parents: Thank you for believing in me even when I didn't believe in myself. Thank you, too, for supporting me in whatever new idea, goal, or dream I had. You have given your entire lives to me and for that I will forever be grateful. You taught me how to live my life to the fullest, how to work hard, how to dream big, and most important, how to love life. I can't ever fully tell you how much admiration and love I have for you both. To my beautiful grandparents who have supported me all the way from Russia, through emails, calls, and now FaceTime: I love you both so much.

To my fiancé, Matt: From the very beginning I knew you loved me for *me*, and not because of my accomplishments. Every day you inspire me to work harder and be a better person. And, you always know how to make me smile and laugh, even when I'm having a bad day. Not only did I find the love of my life, but I also found a best friend. I can't wait to share my life with you, forever. I love you.

To my best friend, my business partner, and my maid of honor, Liz: Thank you for believing in me, when no one else did. Thank you for pushing me to realize I could always be more than just "that gymnast." You have made me set new dreams for myself that I never even thought could be on my vision board, and now we are living those dreams! I'm so excited for our future. Love you gurl. #SHINE

To my best friend, Nina: Ever since I met you when I was ten years old I wanted to be your best friend. I know, I was a little over the top at ten, but you never acted like I was. You loved and supported me from the day we met. From that moment I knew we would be lifelong friends. I still remember seeing you in the stands at the 2008 Olympic Games, cheering for me and wearing a TEAM NASTIA shirt. I can't wait to walk down the aisle with you by my side as one of my bridesmaids. Love you! #ForeverAndAlways

Last but not least, thank you Steve Penny and your wonderful staff at USA Gymnastics: You have believed in me since I made my first junior national team when I was twelve. Your continued support means more than you know. I will forever be grateful in not only representing the Unites States of America, but also for the many opportunities you have given me.

Finally, thank you to Jenna Kutcher, whose amazing photos grace the front and back cover of this book. And, to Lisa, and to Sharlene Martin at Martin Literary Management: Thank you for helping me make my dream of writing a book come true. I couldn't have done it without you.

Chapter One

The night before the all-around gymnastics competition at the 2008 Olympics in Beijing, I had a dream. It was a dream so vivid that I was convinced it was real. My dream was about the next day's competition and I saw myself in the hot pink leotard, matching scrunchy, and the gold eye shadow that I had chosen the night before. Until now we'd had the team competition and we had all worn official red and white Team USA leotards. But the previous night my teammate, Shawn Johnson, and I, who were the only two USA competitors in the all-around, had gotten to choose any leotard we wanted to wear for that event. Pink was my favorite color, and in this particular leotard I felt invincible.

As dreams can sometimes seem a little strange, I saw myself as if watching another person, but the dream was so real that I also experienced it through my own eyes. I remember struggling to find enough strength to succeed on vault, and the frustration I felt in trying to achieve that goal. My strengths as a gymnast had always been grace, style, and flexibility. Strength? Not so much. My longer, leaner body was not typical of most top gymnasts, so I always had to work hard to build strength. Unfortunately for me, to be a great vaulter a gymnast needs to be very strong.

I intensely watched the dream version of myself take a few breaths, and I saw the determined look on her face while I also felt that determination run through my entire body. Then the dream version of me ran, building speed and power as she approached the vaulting "table." She cleared the table with perfect form, and then stuck her landing perfectly, something I had never done in competition. Simultaneously, I felt the impact of the landing in my muscles and bones, the rubber mat under my feet, and the breathless anticipation of the audience in the moment before they burst into applause.

In gymnastics, it is important that whenever the gymnast lands that he or she "sticks" both feet to the mat. Taking even a single step means a deduction in scoring. Not every performance ends in a stuck landing, and in my dream I experienced a rush of excitement in knowing I had stuck the perfect landing.

Next up was the uneven bars. My dream self did a perfect routine, with just a small step on the landing. My balance beam performance, however, was as close to flawless as I could ever imagine. Last was my floor routine, and after another stellar performance, my dad appeared in the sidelines of my dream, and I was so excited and happy that I ran to give him a hug. When I woke up I was sitting up in bed with my arms in the air, still hugging my dream dad.

I turned to orient myself, and saw Shawn sound asleep in the bed next to me. Here we were: two girls, roommates, teammates, who would both be going head-to-head in hopes of achieving our lifelong dream the next day. After that I went back to sleep and slept soundly, but when I woke up the next morning it was with a profound sense of confidence. I had a feeling that whatever had happened in the dream, would happen during this coming day.

I had worked virtually all my life for this one single day; so to say the coming hours were important is the understatement of the century. I was only eighteen years old, and on that morning I felt that much of the rest of my life would rest on the performances I would soon give. I was right, but not exactly in the way I envisioned. More on that later.

Due to NBC's broadcast schedule, the all-around competition started early in the morning of August 15, 2008, and I was dressed, ready, and waiting for the bus by seven AM. My dad, Valeri, was my coach, and he joined me on the bus as we rode with the rest of my team to the huge Beijing National Indoor Stadium. I had never in all my life competed so early in the morning, and it was ironic that the first time I would do so was the most important day of my gymnastic career.

My dad was staying in a hotel outside the Olympic Village with the other coaches, and my mom, Anna, was also in Beijing, but was staying in a different, non-Olympic hotel. I was glad that even if my parents could not stay with my teammates and me in the Olympic Village, that at least my dad could come in during the day and eat with me. That little bit of normalcy in sharing a meal went a long way toward making me feel more relaxed during the most important competition I would ever experience.

My mom often became very nervous when she watched my bigger competitions, and nothing was bigger than the Olympics. She never wanted to pass her nervous vibes along to me, that's why she had decided to visit a temple, rather than watch my competitions that day. To be fair, my mom always asked if I needed her. While I would have loved to have her in the arena, with my blessing, she set out with her cell phone tucked into her purse and my promise to call her with news as soon as I had any.

During my warm-ups I felt the fluttery, nervous feeling that I always got before I competed. Then, after my first practice vault, I took a single step after I landed. My dad then asked me to focus on sticking my next landing and when I did, I realized that my dream of the night before was about to become a reality. It sounds odd, but I knew it with every sense of my being, and that knowledge both filled me with joy, and gave me a big dose of confidence.

Competing on the uneven bars was one of my strengths, and it seemed during my routine that day that I could not make a mistake. And with the exception of the one step that I took on my landing, just as I had done in my dream, I was thrilled with what I had done.

By this time my previous nervousness had completely gone away, and had been replaced with an unusual sense of calm. I was so calm, in fact, that my dad asked if I was okay. I was. I was absolutely, totally, completely okay. In fact, I couldn't remember when I had ever been as confident or focused as I was then.

I was the last one to perform on the beam and, as I had in my dream, I stuck my landing. My final routine in the all-around was floor. Olympic officials were moving us right along, so we all went from one event to the other so quickly that I often wasn't aware of my score in the previous event before I performed the next. This was the case before floor. I felt I had performed well on the beam, and knew I was among the top people in the entire competition, but I was not aware that I was the leader. Sometimes that information is good to have, so you know ahead of time that if you make a mistake, how much that will affect the final placing. This time, however, I did not have that luxury.

Before I began, I reminded myself that I had done this same routine hundreds, possibly even thousands, of times. When it was my turn, I knew that I needed the performance of a lifetime, so I focused and went for it. At the end, I dropped to the floor in my ending pose. When I did, I locked eyes with my dad, who was on the sidelines. Coaches can't talk to gymnasts when they are performing, but this was such an amazing, private moment between my dad and me that words were not needed. I felt all the hours that we had spent together in training during the past twelve years flash before me. At that moment, I was filled with such love and gratitude. Those few seconds allowed us to stare into each other's souls, and in that instant I felt closer to my dad than to anyone else on earth. I was reminded once again that I have the best father in the entire world.

When I walked off the floor, I hugged my dad extra hard and long to make sure this hug, this competition, was real, and that I wasn't caught in the middle of another dream. When the final scores were posted with my name at the top of the leader board, I was overcome with emotion. I had just become an Olympic all-around gold medalist!

The next few minutes passed in a blur. At some point I found a moment to call my mom and was disappointed when she did not pick up. A few minutes later I called again, only to once more reach her voice mail. I ended up texting her: I WON. I LOVE YOU. Even in this private moment a number of cameras were pointed at me. I tried to turn my head away from them, but everywhere I turned cameras were there. I had experienced press attention before, but nothing remotely close to this. I was surrounded.

Before too much time passed, my mom called my dad. She had turned her phone off, as she had not wanted to get updates during the event—from me or anyone else. The level of my mom's nervousness speaks volumes about her love for me, and how much she wanted me to do well.

I was so excited to share this experience with her, and my dad and I would have plenty of time to fill her in later in the day on all the little details she was sure to want to hear. And, of course, she soon would be able to watch the competition during replays on television, and on the DVDs we got from friends and from NBC. I couldn't wait to watch with her.

Soon, I was directed to the raised circles that made up the Olympic podiums for the gold, silver, and bronze presentations and I fought to hold back tears. I was so incredibly honored to represent my country in this competition. Someone handed me a bouquet of red roses, and when the gold medal was dropped over my head and "The Star Spangled Banner" began to play, I tried to sing along, but between trying to breathe and trying to remember the words, I only managed a few lines.

So many thoughts were racing through my mind, it was hard to concentrate on anything. One thought that stuck, though, was of the previous year. I had suffered a severe ankle injury, and many people told me that at eighteen I was too old to compete in world level competitions. Too old at eighteen? Even then I knew there was something wrong with that statement. My life was just starting. I felt from the bottom of my heart that I had not yet peaked in my gymnastics career. There would be many good, positive moments ahead of me—if I could learn *not* to listen to people who didn't have the same goals for me as I had for myself. But that was hard. Positive or negative, we all eventually give in to the words that surround us, and I was no exception.

On one level, the ankle injury and the comments had combined to make me feel like a washed up gymnast held together by a few pieces of tape. But then I consciously decided to make a habit of looking at the situation from another direction. In that direction, I refused to allow other people to define me. That was not as easy as it sounds, however, and I slipped into negative self-talk many times. I knew I had to dig deeper to get those negative comments to start rolling off my back, and to convince myself that it didn't matter what negative people said. And dig deeper I did.

I began to tell myself that the only opinions that mattered were the opinions of the people who supported me every day at the gym, in school, and at home. What was important was having people around me every day that I could trust and be myself with. Fortunately, I had many of those people. When I realized all of that, I consciously re-committed myself to my goal of reaching the Olympics.

I remembered all of this in bits and flashes as our national anthem played, then I raised the bouquet of red roses to acknowledge the cheering crowd. As soon as I stepped off the platform, I found myself once again surrounded by reporters, cameras, and microphones. Everyone wanted to hear about my performances from my perspective. It was all quite overwhelming, but it was all very exciting, too.

The emotion of the day did not stop there. I later learned that my mom had gone to a Buddhist monastery that morning. She believes that there is an invisible bond that always stretches between a mother and her children, no matter where they are. My mom wanted to do everything she could to stay calm, so as not to translate any of her nervousness for me through that invisible thread.

At the monastery, she took part in a beautiful and peaceful ceremony, one that was filled with quiet music and dozens of white candles. During and immediately after, she felt quite at peace, but soon her nervousness crept back in. She checked her watch and realized it was far too soon to have any news. Then, looking around, my mom saw a day spa next door to the monastery. How convenient, she thought, and she went in.

Even though my mom spoke no Chinese, and the people inside the spa spoke no English, she was able to convey that she wanted a massage. Then she turned off her phone as she relaxed into the kneading hands of the masseuse. After, and back out on the street, she turned on her phone to find all kinds of texts. My mom told me how afraid she was to look at them because she did not want to hear the news, whatever it was, from anyone but me. As long as she didn't look at the texts, the dream was still alive. She also knew how hard I had worked and wanted so badly for me to win. But, as she had often said, as long as you do your best, that's what matters. You can't control the outcome. She would always be proud of me, regardless of the final result.

My mom knew that eventually she'd have to be brave, so she said a quick prayer, then skipped over all of the texts until she came to mine. I later learned that when she saw my text, she jumped into the first taxi that came along, and then started to cry huge, loud, sobs of emotion. I had won. I had really and truly won.

While no other moment in my life can compare with winning a gold medal at the Olympics—for either my family or me—it turned out that this was not the defining moment in my life. That happened four years later.

Chapter Two

One reason I felt so proud to represent the United States at the Olympics was that America is my adopted country. Like my parents, I was born in Russia, but after the fall of the former Soviet Union in December of 1991, my mom and dad wanted a new start, so they came to America and first settled in New Orleans, Louisiana, because they had friends there.

I was two and a half at the time, so I don't remember the move, but I can only imagine how hard it must have been for them. My mother's side of the family is especially close, and to move that far away to a different culture and a new country must have been hard on all of them. In addition, both of my parents were gymnasts and had represented their country many times in the sport. For their country to essentially no longer exist, well, I am sure there was a lot of sadness involved.

Both my mom and dad wanted to make the move, though, because they wanted a better life for me than what they'd had growing up. During their careers, they had each traveled here to the United States to represent the Soviet Union: my mom at Princeton University in 1987, and my dad on a gymnastics tour. My dad had also come to the US just a few months before the fall of the USSR, to the 1991 World Gymnastics Championships in Indianapolis, where he won a bronze medal in the all-around competition. Both of my parents thought America would give them, and me, the best chance at a new start.

Being together were the two most important things in the world to my parents. My dad, Valeri, was born in 1966 in the city of Aktyubinsk, which is in the northwestern part of what is now Kazakhstan. He started his gymnastic career when he was six or seven, after he followed his older brother, Sasha, to gymnastics practice one day. After seeing young Valeri hiding near a corner of the sidelines, Sasha's coach asked my dad to show him what he could do.

It turned out that my dad was a better gymnast than Sasha, and when he was eleven, my dad moved away to live with his coach and his coach's family. The two-hour plane ride to his coach's home meant that my dad had to spend long periods of time away from his parents and brother. My dad had a lot of talent and really wanted to be a gymnast, that was his passion. So, like other athletes in the Soviet Union's elite athletic system, he had to pay the price of leaving his family to pursue his dream.

Kids, even young ones, lived with coaches and only saw their families for a short period of time every few months. For centuries the Russian people have had a rich history in the arts, and in artistic sports such as gymnastics. Their culture and tradition valued the arts so much, that they took care to develop these talents in their youngest citizens, their children. That meant total immersion from a young age, and that's why the Soviet Union for decades had dominated international competitions.

I know that my dad missed his family, but they wrote letters back and forth. This was long before the Internet, and a long-distance phone call was quite expensive. It was all worth it though, because my dad became quite successful. As a teen, my dad mastered skills that no one else in the world was doing, and by 1988, when he was twenty-two, he had become a four-time Olympic medalist. At the '88 Games in Seoul, Korea, he won a gold medal in the team competition as part of the Soviet Team, and an individual gold medal for the high bar. He also won silver medals in the individual competition for the parallel bars and the all-around.

My dad stayed with the Soviet team until 1991, when the Soviet Union dissolved. Then he competed for his native Kazakhstan and retired from competition after the 1994 Asian Games. He has been successful in his coaching career, too, and among many other honors, was named International Coach of the Year in 2002 and 2004, International Gymnastics Coach of the Year in 2009, and was inducted into the International Gymnastics Hall of Fame in 2005.

My mom was also on the Soviet gymnastics team, but was fortunate enough to be able to live at home with her parents, as her coach lived nearby. My mom was born in Moscow in 1970, and was the 1987 world champion in rhythmic gymnastics/clubs. Rhythmic gymnastics is a sport that gracefully integrates objects like clubs, hoops, long ribbons, and ropes into the routines, and the routines themselves are a mixture of gymnastics, ballet, and other forms of dance. My mom also earned world championship bronze medals in competition with the hoops and also with rope.

My mom and dad met in 1987 on a forty-city gymnastics tour of Australia and New Zealand, and a relationship between them was encouraged my dad's long-time friend and current business partner, Yevgeny Marchenko. My dad and Yevgeny had met each other at a Soviet national team training camp when my dad was thirteen. Yevgeny, who has become like a second dad to me, was born in Latvia and was a sports acrobatics gymnast who won five world champion titles, four European champion titles and was a national USSR champion. Even after he had tried to set up my mom and dad several times, my mom was still not interested. At all. In fact, she said no many times to possible dates with my dad.

Her reasons were many. Although both she and my dad were world travelers when it came to gymnastics and sports, my mom admits to being naïve when it came to the world of dating. She was uncomfortable with small talk and nervous at the thought of spending time alone with a boy. So, she said no.

However, my mom and dad were part of a group of athletes who hung out together after their performances on the tour. After a while, she began to see my dad as a steady man of strong character, a reliable guy whom she could trust, and she relented about the dating. The rest is history. My parents were married on December 27, 1988, not all that long after they met, and I came along on October 30, 1989. I was to become their only child.

My full name is Anastasia Valeryevna Liukin, although I rarely use my real first name. In Russia, Nastia (or Naast-ya, as it is pronounced in Russian) is a common nickname for girls who are named Anastasia. My middle name was a given. Traditionally, Russian names have three parts. Besides the first and last name, the middle name is usually the child's father's name with "ovich" or "evich" added to the end of a boy's name, and "ovna" or "evna" added to the end of a girl's. As my dad's first name is Valeri, my middle name became Valeryevna.

Actually, my parents could have named me anything, but my name, my middle name in particular, is a shining example of how important country and heritage were to my mom and dad.

By the time I arrived, my parents were living in a cramped, two bedroom apartment in a fifth-floor walk-up in central Moscow with my maternal grandparents, Olga and Vladimir Kochnev. Both of my grandparents had good jobs. My grandfather was a medical supply rep for a company that sold supportive arm, leg, and back braces, and my grandmother was an engineer who at one time worked with atoms. Their good jobs and good standing in the community meant that even though the apartment was tiny, it was in a relatively safe area. During that period of time, housing of any kind was almost impossible to get in Moscow, even for people with decent jobs, and even Olympic champions.

Plus, my parents were very young. My mom was only seventeen when she and my dad met. She was married at eighteen and was just nineteen when I was born. My dad was only a few years older, and he was away a lot, training, as he was still competing for the Soviet national team. He also had a place in Kazakhstan near his own family, and tried to make up for lost time by visiting them when he could. So it was good that my mom and I could be with my grandparents, because my dad was away so much of the time.

Even though life in Russia after I was born still involved competitive gymnastics for my dad, my mom retired as soon as she heard I was on the way. While we still lived in Russia, she was a stay-at-home mom. In talking to my parents, grandparents, and even my great-grandparents, I have been told that we were a typical Russian family, and that we were together as much as we could be with my dad still actively training and competing. As the only grandchild on both my mom and dad's side of the family, I was a very special addition. By 1991, however, there was a lot of unrest in the Soviet Union, and our country fell apart on December 26, 1991, the day before my parents' third wedding anniversary. The fall of the country meant the Soviet gymnastics team was gone, too. My dad knew he had to support my mom and me somehow, and he had many offers for coaching jobs in Germany and other areas throughout Europe.

At that time, though, there was little money to be found in Europe in the field of coaching, and the republics (or states) that had made up the former Soviet Union had not yet gotten organized enough to think about elite or Olympic-level athletic teams. Russian gymnasts were in great demand outside of Europe though, since at that time the Russian gymnasts were the best in the world. Other countries wanted to take advantage of the skill and knowledge the Soviet system had produced.

It was time to start a new phase in life. My dad briefly considered joining my grandfather in his medical supply business, but moving into coaching was a natural progression for him. Also, for many years he and Yevgeny had dreamed of owning a gym together, a place where they could coach other athletes and help other gymnasts realize their dreams. Immediately after the fall of the Soviet Union, Yevgeny, along with his own wife and young daughter, had followed his former coach to New Orleans, Louisiana, where he got a job coaching at a gym. A few months later, my parents and I followed.

I sometimes wonder what my life would have been like if my mom and dad had made a different choice. Who would I be now if I had been raised, for example, in Germany? Each of our choices has a ripple effect in our lives, and in the lives of people around us, and I am glad that my parents carefully considered all aspects of this important move before they made it.

When we arrived, my parents and I had only a few suitcases and enough money to buy a very old and well-used car. That was it. After living with Yevgeny and his family for a month or so, we found a small apartment, and both my mom and dad found jobs coaching at a different gym than the one where Yevgeny worked. Fortunately, the gym also offered childcare for employees, and I happily spent my days getting to know my first American friends.

One of the hardest things about the move for my parents was the language. We all, of course, spoke Russian. My parents are both intelligent people but had learned little English along the way. As you can imagine, learning the intricacies of a second language can be very difficult, and it took my mom and dad years before speaking English was an integrated part of their life.

Fortunately, gymnastics is a very physical sport, and even though my mom and dad did not know very many words in English, they could still coach by using body language and by physically demonstrating with their own body, for instance, that a straighter knee, or squarer shoulders were needed. It is also a good thing that a smile and a high-five are universal signals of success. American kids are also very accepting and gracious, so the language barrier was not as difficult for them as it might have been for an adult.

The language transition was easier for me. At two and a half, I was still learning to speak Russian. I have heard people say that the earlier a child learns a second language, the easier it is for him or her to become bi-lingual. That was true for me. My parents now both speak English very well, but both have a trace of an accent. I don't have an accent, although I am still fluent in Russian.

I love that I can speak two languages, and that culturally I have a foot in both worlds. Anytime a person can broaden his or her horizons, there comes an opportunity for learning, meeting people, and new experiences. I am so grateful to my parents that they not only came here to the United States, but that they raised me immersed in both American and Russian culture.

What courage my parents had. They landed in New Orleans in the middle of February, and it just so happened that it was Mardi Gras week. Mardi Gras is an annual week-long, carnival-like celebration that is held throughout the city. There are loud parties day and night in businesses and clubs, and even carnival parades in the streets. You can imagine the chaos that surrounded their arrival. Years later, my mom told me that at the time, she and my dad thought all of America was as shocking and surreal as Mardi Gras—every day—and they worried about raising me in such a wild and crazy environment. Whenever I feel that life has become too difficult, I remember all that my parents went through to achieve their dreams and give me a better life, and I draw strength from how well they met those challenges.

Some years ago I asked my dad why America? Why not Canada or England, Japan or Brazil? There are so many countries throughout the world that they could have chosen. Why here?

The main reason, he said, was that Yevgeny was here in the United States, and that the support of his friendship, along with other friends, was important to him and to my mother. He reminded me that he and my mom and Yevgeny had always wanted to open their own gym. That was their dream. Then he added something very interesting. "In Russia," he added, "that would not have been possible, as most businesses were owned and operated by the government."

In America, anyone can open and run a business. That was an exciting thought to my dad, who thought of the United States as the land of opportunity. I am so glad that, for my parents, opportunities were plentiful. They just had to keep their eyes and ears open, and be proactive in looking for chances.

Soon after we arrived, Yevgeny, my parents, and Yevgeny's coach began scouting around for a place to open a gym. They looked in Atlanta, since it was much larger than New Orleans, but after multiple trips, nothing came of it. It didn't help that none of them had any credit history in the United States, or a large sum of money to put down toward a lease on a building. My dad and Yevgeny even brought their Olympic and world championship medals to several banks. Sadly, as impressive as they were, they weren't enough to secure a loan. In early summer of 1993, more than a year after we moved to New Orleans, a mutual friend asked my dad and Yevgeny to have a look around Dallas, Texas.

My dad and Yevgeny both remember driving northeast from Dallas to the suburb of Plano and seeing school after school, thirty-two schools in all, every one of them filled with kids. Surely at least some of them had an interest in gymnastics? They also saw hundreds of houses being built and a number of corporate headquarters for large, national businesses. It didn't take a genius to figure out that this area was just waiting to explode. This area of Texas, they thought, could be a huge hotspot for gymnastics, and they saw infinite possibilities for the future.

New Orleans had been wonderful and welcoming, but the climate had been much hotter and more humid than we had been used to in Moscow. While Texas was hot, too, it was a drier heat. Plus, my parents had encountered some cultural differences in New Orleans. They had been raised in a culture that valued a "do it now, get it done" work ethic. New Orleans, for all its charm, was far more laid back. My parents found it hard to understand that the families of the kids they coached put more emphasis on celebrations such as Mardi-Gras, than in getting their kids to the gym. It was not a culture that was any better or worse than what my mom and dad grew up in, it was just different, and they had a hard time adjusting.

New Orleans had been wonderful and welcoming, but my parents and Yevgeny made the decision to relocate to Plano, and after they arrived they found a large, empty warehouse that had once housed a grocery store. After signing the lease, they found they did not have enough money to actually open the gym. They met with bank after bank, and with one investor after the other, but money was very hard to come by. Another problem was meeting all the codes and regulations that were needed to pass inspections. Build a dividing wall? It sounded simple, but it took two months to get it up, and to get it to pass inspection.

In the meantime, my parents and Yevgeny wanted to advertise that they would soon be opening their great new gym. There was no advertising budget, however, so they found a bed sheet and some paint. Then they painted NEW GYM OPENING SOON and the phone number on the sheet and hung it on the front of the building. The phone began to ring.

Before they could open, however, money began to get tight, and in desperation my dad and Yevgeny filled out pizza delivery applications. They never actually started those jobs though, because there was one last resort. My dad flew back to Kazakhstan and sold absolutely everything he had there. It didn't come to a huge amount, but it was enough to get the gym open. Finally, nearly eight months after they began work on it, my parents' dream became a reality in February of 1994. The day they opened, my mom, dad, and Yevgeny combined had only had three hundred dollars left in the bank.

The gym was named WOGA, short for the World Olympics Gymnastics Academy. Besides all their good hopes for my future, all of my mom and dad's hopes and dreams were tied up in this gym. Of course they'd had years to plan for just the kind of gym they wanted. After careful thought and consideration they had decided on the exact environment they wanted to offer. In addition to training Olympic hopefuls, my parents wanted to offer a fun, friendly place for all kids to learn about and improve their fitness in a positive environment.

By the time the gym opened for enrollment close to 150 kids had signed up, and my parents were thrilled, relived, and excited to begin living their new dream. It wasn't easy at first, though. No start-up business is. Success requires long hours and many sacrifices, but both my mom and dad were more than willing to do whatever it took to make their new gym succeed.

Part of that was cutting down on costs whenever possible, and that involved me. Daycare, even back then, was expensive and to put it frankly, my parents could not afford it. My mom's coaching skills and managerial talents were needed every day at the gym, so besides the financial consideration, she could not stay home with me due to work.

Of course both of my parents wanted the best for me, and experts say that the best for young children is to be around family. This is where I think my parents felt a huge loss in their new country. Back home in Russia there had been grandparents and great-grandparents to help with my childcare. Here, there were no relatives at all. No aunts or uncles, no cousins to call when life became overwhelming. Other than Yevgeny and his family, there was absolutely no one to fall back on to ease the load if

I got sick, or just had a bad day, as young children sometimes have.

This particular challenge could have been a huge problem, but out of desperation, miracle solutions often arrive. With nowhere else to put me, my parents began bringing me to the gym. Not occasionally, but all day, every day. It was a brilliant idea in many ways. First and foremost, I was with my parents all the time. This allowed us to forge an incredibly tight bond that exists still today.

Then, because I was an only child with no cousins or other relatives to play with, I got to see, meet, and play with all kinds of kids at the gym. It was the perfect place for me to learn how to socialize, and to get to know many different kinds of kids. I still love to meet new people and know that my early years in my parents' gym taught me to feel comfortable with people of many different backgrounds and cultures. Those early years also taught me that any opportunity to meet someone new, especially someone who might be from a different country, culture, age, or race, is an opportunity worth taking.

Finally, I got to watch older kids learn to tumble, and perform routines on the uneven bars and the balance beam. Some of my earliest memories revolve around watching these older kids, and I became fascinated by the interesting ways they could move their bodies. I loved watching as they eventually put a sequence of seemingly unrelated moves together to create a fluid, graceful work of art. To me, it was like magic.

While I was being readily entertained by watching the older kids, my mom and dad were watching me with more than a little unease. My parents had not only never envisioned a life of gymnastics for me, they had never even considered it. This was because they knew how much hard work and sacrifice needed to happen for someone to be successful in the competitive side of the sport. It was important to them that I have a well-rounded upbringing, and that I experience a lot of different activities. I, however, had other ideas.

Before long I was trying out some basic tumbling moves on my own. Even at the ages of three and four, I loved to cartwheel across a room and imagine music in my head as I put a routine together. My parents would look up and there I was, hanging on the bars, jumping on the trampoline, or walking on the low balance beam. I begged my dad and some of the other coaches who worked at the gym to let me try vaulting, and I pleaded with my mom to let me learn with the older girls I idolized so much.

Gymnastics was something I really, *really* wanted to try. My parents did not push me into the sport. I pushed myself. From day one, both my mom and my dad made sure I knew I could quit anytime I wanted and could try any other activity I wanted. But all I wanted was gymnastics.

At my very young age they sensed that I had at least a little bit of talent for the sport. Of course, both of my parents had been the best in the world in their respective activities, so it followed genetically that I might have some ability as well. However, even if I had been a complete klutz on the floor I still think my mom and dad would have let me try. That's what a person's early years are all about: trying new things and learning from your failures, as well as your successes. There is something important to learn in every experience, and there are many good lessons that can help you in the future.

My parents taught me to learn from everything I did, in and out of the sport, and that is something I take with me today. Do you like sushi, for example? You don't know until you try it. Are you artistic? Musical? Good at figuring out how to make things? My parents taught me that if you have an interest in something then you should follow that interest to see where it goes. My one and only interest from the time I was about three until I became an Olympic champion was gymnastics. I do not regret any second I spent in the gym or in competition, and as you'll see, I still had quite a variety of experiences during my childhood.

Chapter Three

As soon as I started in classes at the gym, I realized that I never wanted to leave. I started with weekly classes and progressed from there. Soon, I found that I loved everything about gymnastics, as well as our gym. From our shiny white walls to the high white ceilings, to the thick, cushy blue mats, the mirrored wall, the rows and rows of equipment, and the coaches and other kids, I was in heaven.

My mom was my first coach and I loved it so much that I wanted to sleep at the gym and wear my leotard all day and all night, every day of the week. Yevgeny also coached me some, as did Sergei Pakanich, who was one of the first coaches my parents hired. Sergei was a member of the Latvian National Team from 1978-1988, and was champion of the Republic of Latvia from 1978-1988. From day one, my mom and dad and Yevgeny made a habit of hiring top gymnasts as our coaches. Even today you will see a number of Olympians and former national and world champions teaching and training kids at WOGA.

I am so thankful that I found something I was so passionate about at such a young age. And, I realize that not everyone has the luxury of having a dad who is an expert in his or her area of interest. I was very fortunate that my dad was one of the top coaches in the world. But even if that had not been the case, I know I would have found a way to spend time in a gym and learn about the sport I loved so much.

There is an old saying, "where there is a will there is a way," which basically means if you want something badly enough you will find a way to reach your goal. I learned to never let anything stop me from reaching my goals. Success might not come in the time frame that I wanted or expected, and my actual success often turned out to be much different from how I initially envisioned it, but I always thought creatively to find a way to reach each goal I set for myself, and then worked hard. Success in some way, shape, or form usually came.

Sadly for me, I did not get my wish to be in the gym 24/7, but looking back I can see that was a good thing. Balance in life is needed and necessary. My parents wisely initiated a rule that when we were home, we did not talk about what happened that day in the gym. We were a regular little family at home and spoke of regular, non-work related topics.

Our gym, WOGA, was in Plano, Texas, and we first lived in an apartment, and then in a duplex nearby. We eventually moved about fifteen minutes away to the small town of Parker. Parker is best known for being the home of Southfork Ranch, the ranch that was home to the popular television shows *Dallas* (1978-1991 and 2012-2014). The physical separation from my beloved gym was good for me, but my thoughts were rarely far away. I couldn't wait until the next day when I could go back and learn some more.

Some nights I even refused to take off my leotard and my parents had to wait until I fell asleep to exchange it for pajamas. I dreamed about the large banners and magazine covers of other gymnasts that were hanging from the walls at WOGA and it moti-vated me. Maybe someday I, too, could be on that wall.

Before I even began pre-K, my young life took on a regular routine. I'd get up in the morning, go to the gym with my parents, go home, eat dinner, do a few chores around the house, then go to sleep. Sleep was always an important activity in our family, as my parents knew that no one operates at their best if they are tired.

For me, making sure I got enough sleep was extremely important. I needed to be at my top game, and learned when I was very young that enough quality sleep was a necessary part of life, and of reaching any goal.

The months of June, July, and August are some of the busiest for the elite, or top level, gymnasts. Even though I was not yet competing at any major level, my dad had to be at many of the big competitions because he coached other athletes who competed at that level. Between summer competitions, though, most years when I was young we went back to Russia to visit relatives. A few times my dad could not get away, so my mom and I went by ourselves and made it a girls' trip.

We went in the summer not only because I was out of school then, but because Moscow in the winter can be brutal. During the winter, my grandparents often came to visit us in Texas. I was blessed not only to have my maternal grandparents, but I also had four great-grandparents, all on my mother's side. Not every child gets to know even one great-grandparent and I treasured every moment with all four of mine.

I am still struck by how supportive they were of me. When I began to compete, one of my great-grandfathers, my maternal grandmother's father, Boris Berdnikov, wrote me a long letter. In it, he made a detailed technical drawing of how I should hold the uneven bars during one of my routines. I was struck then by his interest in me, and still cherish his letter today. He had not been a gymnast, but he was incredibly smart and was the kind of man who instinctively knew how things worked, or how they should look.

His army training might have been part of that, as he reached the rank of colonel. He also, until the age of ninety, wrote a regular newspaper column that detailed intricate chess moves that he had developed. That man was the rock of our family. I still have his letter and his drawing. I wonder how many of us have letters written specifically to us from a great-grandparent?

I only met my dad's parents once, when I was a baby, and sadly do not remember that encounter at all. The separation between my dad and his family had a lot to do with the early training my dad had so far away from his home. There was never any contention between them; they just had not spent enough hours together to develop a strong bond, as many other families do. Then his parents both died fairly young, so the opportunity for me to get to know them was lost. When I was about twelve, my uncle Sasha moved with his wife, Irina, to the Dallas area to work at the gym. He had not had as big a career in gymnastics as my dad, but he also had participated in track and field events. His move to Dallas was the first opportunity I'd had to really get to know anyone from my dad's side of the family, and I welcomed it.

As I have grown to be an adult I have come to realize the importance of family. In addition to your actual family, I have found that "family" can include anyone who has loved you and supported you in your goals for a long period of time, and who is also a person whom you trust. I have met many people like my dad, who do not have many biological family members close by, or who for whatever reason have had to distance themselves from their families. Those people inevitably seek out other kinds of "family" who then become as close or closer than the real thing. My dad was right. Support from family and good friends is very important and I have learned to choose wisely when it comes to my closest friends. Today, I only allow people who support and encourage me in a positive way into my life.

On our trips back to Russia, I also got to visit the apartment where we lived when I was born. My grandparents lived there until I was a teenager, so that was where we stayed when we were in Moscow. As I grew older I could see that everything about their building was old and worn down, from the appliances to the flooring. It makes sense, as Moscow is a very old city, many centuries older than America, so the buildings are very historic.

I was, during my younger years, struck by the difference between my grandparents' apartment in Moscow and where I lived. People say that everything is bigger in Texas, and that must be true, as most of the housing I saw in Russia consisted of very small spaces. Moscow reminds me a lot of New York City, a place that I have come to adore. In both places, people walk everywhere, or take the subway or another form of public transportation. Few people have cars. Housing units are in the form of apartments and the apartments are very small, and often they are outdated.

When I was young, we lived in a one bedroom apartment, then moved to a two bedroom duplex, and finally to our own house. Later on, my parents bought some land and built their dream home. But even the one bedroom apartment we had in Texas was light years ahead of my grandparents' apartment in Moscow, in terms of size, amenities, and convenience.

But the age or looks of an apartment, a building, or a city did not matter to me. What mattered was what was inside all of that. In this case, in Moscow, it was my grandparents. I loved spending time with them, and still do. Those times in Russia were precious to me, especially when I got older and began competing more in the summer. Due to my travel schedule it became increasingly difficult to get to Moscow to see everyone, so I enjoyed the moments we did see them even more. I was so excited to learn that my grandparents recently purchased a home not too far from where my parents live, making it possible to visit with them even more often.

As I grew older, my parents took me to a gym where I could train in when we were in Moscow. I loved gymnastics so much that I never wanted to miss a single day. Dynamo was a huge and well-respected Russian gym that also had sentimental value for my family because my dad had trained there. My parents were long-time friends with the owners and coaches, and one year I got to train for a week with their team. It was a lot of fun, and because I was bi-lingual, communication between the coaches, other girls, and me was never a problem.

Some years my grandparents came to visit us in Texas. They always tried to be there for New Year's Eve, but sometimes also came during the summer. I loved that when they visited, they got to see my room, see where I went to school, and visit the gym. Those visits were always exciting for me, but in another way they were more relaxed, as I got to stay in my home environment, and was not tired from all the travel.

As much as I loved the gym, I greatly anticipated my first day of school. All my life I had looked up to the "big girls," those older girls who could perform far more advanced gymnastics moves than I could. I wanted to be just like those girls in every way, and that included going to school. When I started pre-K and kindergarten, it was at small private school, but by first grade I had moved to a public school in Plano, Wells Elementary.

In our family education was very important, and I wanted to absorb everything I learned in school almost as much as I wanted to absorb everything at the gym. So many times I heard my dad say, "An education will stick with you for the rest of your life, but you never know how long gymnastics will stay with you." I would come to find that his words were very true.

I found that I liked all of the subjects in my early years of school, but I was especially drawn to math because I could closely relate it to gymnastics. Completing a gymnastics routine involves a lot of counting. Take three steps, twist two times, make one graceful hand gesture, and then repeat four times. In addition, math involved distance, angles, and measurements: run ten feet, make a 90-degree turn, then turn my head ten degrees.

Then there was the intricate scoring that comes with competitive gymnastics. Sometimes one thousandth of a point separated the winner from the second place finisher. I wanted to learn how those scored were calculated, and how I could incorporate the scores of the girls who performed before I did into my last-minute strategy. Could I play it on the safe side during a difficult skill, or did I need to go all out?

Progressing through the lower grades, I found that I could relate many of my subjects to what was going on in my gymnastics life. Geography and history helped me learn about the places I traveled to compete. Learning solid writing and speaking skills helped me communicate my thoughts and feelings with coaches, kids I trained with, and other competitors. Science helped me better understand my body, and how bad weather might interrupt travel plans for a meet. Yes, school was important, but always, I anticipated the end of the school day when I could go to the gym, watch the big girls, and practice.

After school and the gym, I was usually home by seven o'clock. We had a family dinner of lean meat and vegetables, and then I did my homework and went to bed early. Sleep, as I said, was of huge importance because I had to get up and do it all again the next day.

I did have a few challenges that other students might not have had, though. While my parents' English speaking skills had improved over the few years we had been in the United States, they still did not read or write well in English. And, we usually still spoke Russian at home, although both my mom and dad used what English they had at the gym. I remember sitting at our little kitchen table teaching them English words and letters as I learned them. My mom and dad peered over my shoulder while I practiced writing my letters, and when I read aloud such basic words as boy, toy, dog, and cat. Then they practiced the same words and letters on their own.

My parents often watched *Barney* and *Sesame Street* on television with me, as it helped them improve their English. As I learned, so did they. I am sure children of many immigrant parents do this very same thing, but I did not know any other immigrant children. My beautiful but unusual name, my parents' accents, and their lack of English speaking and writing skills made me feel different when all I wanted to do was fit in and be like everyone else. Already I was "the girl from Russia." I especially felt bad when some of the meaner kids at school called me "Nasty" instead of "Nastia." It wasn't the word that gave me bad feelings as much as the way it was said so hatefully. I don't want to claim that I was bullied, but any word or action that makes a person feel unwelcome or unsafe is a form of bullying, and we all need to make an effort to put an end to it.

Even though when I was young, seven or eight years old, the mean kids made me cry with their cruel words, I refused to dwell on it. I had a good group of friends who liked me and were kind, and the gym was always there. As soon as I stepped inside it, I forgot any tension I might have felt at school and concentrated on the training that I loved so much. So in the end, I shook off the meanness of a very few children and lost myself in the wonderful routine of gymnastics.

Month in and month out, I trained six days a week, with Sundays off for rest and recuperation. It was definitely a busy life for a young girl who was not yet ten years old, but my parents also wanted me to have as normal a life as possible. The only trouble with that was that I did not cooperate very well in their efforts.

I was invited to a lot of sleepovers, which usually are exciting events for kids. I tried them a few times and soon decided they were not for me. In my school, most of the sleepovers happened from after school on Fridays and went on into Saturday mornings. That meant I'd miss some training sessions. Plus, if I did get to the gym on Saturday morning after a sleepover, I was so tired that I was not able to do my best. On my own, I decided that sleepovers were not for me. I'd rather spend my time practicing and reaching toward my goal.

I want to make it clear that this was totally my decision. There was such a passion in my heart for gymnastics that I still wanted to spend every free, waking moment at the gym. I loved working on new skills, the smell of the chalk that I used on my hands when I went up on the bars, and the friendships I had with other gymnasts. In addition, the sense of accomplishment that I felt when I mastered a new skill or put a new routine together was like no other. For me, all of that beat a sleepover, hands down.

When I was about nine, my parents thought I should explore other interests, so my mom signed me up for piano lessons. My mom had taken piano lessons when she was young, so maybe that's why that particular activity was chosen. I know it was an effort to round me out as a person, but I hated piano. I absolutely hated it. Part of it was that I had a really great Russian teacher, but she was as serious about practicing the piano as I was about training in the gym. All I could think of was the time I spent in front of the keyboard was time I was not spending in the gym. I had no interest in learning the notes or anything about the keyboard, and I cried after every lesson. After three or four times I was ecstatic when my mom said I could let it go.

We all learned a few things from that experience. The first was that my interest in gymnastics was not a phase, as my parents thought it might be. I was very serious about taking it as far as I could. Then I learned that while I liked listening to music, I had little interest in creating it. But, I might not have known that if I had not tried it. The same is true for the sleepovers. How would I know that I'd rather be in the gym if I hadn't tried something else? The other important lesson here was that my parents also saw how my commitment to my chosen sport went. Now they, too, knew that I was in it for as far as it would take me.

If you, however, happen to love playing piano, then that is exactly what you should do. If you adore playing chess, are fascinated by biology, or can't wait to get home to create new programs on your computer, then go for it. It is important to find a way to become as immersed as possible in your interests. And, it's okay if those interests change from time to time. My passion for gymnastics never wavered, but if it had, I have no doubt that my parents would have found a way to involve me in whatever my new interest was. All they wanted was for me to be happy, and I think that is true of most moms and dads, spouses and siblings.

You might think that giving me such happiness was easy for my parents, but that is not exactly true. Yes, they owned a gym and my dad was my coach. But, my parents were still in the early stages of getting their gym off the ground. Just a few years earlier they had come here to the United States with next to nothing. Even though my parents were in the business, so to speak, they still had to pay for my leotards, and entry fees to competitions. As I got older, there were travel costs, and fees for appointments for massages, acupuncture, and chiropractic care. Competing at the top levels of any sport, or any interest, can be expensive.

One other huge benefit from our gymnastics lifestyle was the family unit that we eventually came to think of as "Team Liukin." Every day I saw what my parents did to keep our little family going. I saw firsthand their individual challenges and struggles with the business, and in their day-to-day lives. That gave me a unique and profound respect for my mom and dad, especially since they were my primary coaches.

Gymnastics competitions in the United States are divided into levels from one to ten. Combined, levels one through six make up the compulsory levels, where every gymnast performs the same routine in each event. Skills are added to each level until you get to ten. Past Level 10 there is an elite level, which is where the national, world champion, and Olympic athletes are.

My mom, Yevgeny, and Sergei coached me until I was about ten, and had reached Level 6. After that my dad took over my coaching. By the time I was twelve, I had reached the elite level. It must have been a delicate balance for them, walking that line between parent and coach, but our rule about no talking of gymnastics at home helped. At home, my parents were just my parents, and I was just their daughter.

Whether coach or parent, I have always respected my mom and dad. So many kids do not get along with their parents and I think that is sad. For better or worse, parents are people, too, and they each have issues that they deal with as adults, separate and apart from being parents. One mom might be stressed from caring for her own parents. A dad might be having trouble with his boss. Those events can influence how much energy—or how many smiles—a parent has to give at home. Plus, another parent truly might not understand how important soccer is to his daughter, or even how the game of soccer is played, if he had been president of his high school chess club. Different people, different interests, but it is still important to honor and respect those differences and the accomplishments that come with them.

Of course, kids need to be kids and parents need to draw on their life experiences to do what's best for their children and their family. Even though adults don't always get it right, a child should understand that for the most part, parents try. I was able to get to know my parents as people long before many other kids did. That often only happens after a child becomes an adult. What a wonderful world it would be if parents and kids learned to support and respect each other, differences and all, and if parents and kids also acted in a way that was deserving of such respect. If I have one wish here, it is that kids and parents increase their efforts to understand each other. Family is so important.

Chapter Four

As much as I liked public school, by the time my fourth grade year ended it had become obvious that public education was not working for me. My grades were very good and I liked my teachers and friends, but I began traveling to competitions and missed a lot of school. Our public school system was not set up for a child athlete, or any child who was artistically gifted and needed to practice or train more than the average student.

A number of kids who trained at WOGA went to a private school called Spring Creek Academy. This was a private school for highly motivated, gifted, and talented students in Plano, not too far from the gym. The best part? My dad helped start the school.

My mom and dad, and Yevgeny, had grown up in the very successful Soviet system where athletes (and musicians and other creative kids) trained twice a day. There was a morning training, followed by lunch and school, followed by a second, afternoon training. My parents and the other coaches at WOGA felt they could be successful with that formula here in the United States, too. But, the schools here, or at least the ones in Plano, did not allow for that kind of a schedule.

My dad began talking to parents of kids who trained at WOGA about his idea of starting a school for athletes and other talented kids. A number of the moms and dads liked his idea very much. Even if their child did not make it to the Olympics or even if they did not become a national or world champion, most of the parents knew that if their son or daughter reached a Level 10 in gymnastics ability, he or she had a good chance of getting a full scholarship to any college or university in the country that offered a gymnastics program. Plus, their kids would have learned a lot about time management, responsibility, poise, teamwork, goal setting, and dedication, all things every person needs to help them get through life.

Spring Creek Academy was founded in the mid-1990s with very small classes in leased space across the street from the gym. The hired teachers were more like tutors for home school students and all of the kids came from WOGA. That scenario quickly changed. The idea was so successful, that land was purchased and a small, brick school building was built just three blocks or so from the gym. Then the school became accredited with the state and kids began pouring in from other gyms and from other artistic areas. By the time I got there several years later, in addition to gymnasts, a number of the students were musicians, skaters, actors, tennis players, and dancers. A second small building was built, and then a third.

Class sizes were, and are, small (there were only about two hundred kids total from kindergarten through twelfth grade when I went there) and I only needed to go to school from twelve-thirty until three in the afternoon. Just two and a half hours of school every day sounds like a piece of cake, but trust me, it wasn't. We had to learn everything in that short time frame that other students learn in an entire day. I was excited about the new school, though, because many of my friends went there and it put me back into the gym in the mornings.

Plus, when I traveled to a competition or a training camp I sometimes was gone for a week or longer. Then, I struggled to fit back into my classes. In public school this was more of a problem than I hoped it would be at Spring Creek Academy. Because the Spring Creek student body was filled with students who were exceptional musicians, actors, and athletes, being away from school was a regular thing and the teachers there were more able to fit the students back in when they returned. I would come to find that it was still a struggle for me to reconnect with my schedule and classes, but not as much of a struggle as it had been in public school.

So, the fall of my fifth grade year gave me a new school and a new schedule. I'd get up about six-thirty every morning. I hate to admit it, but I wasn't a big breakfast eater then. That's mostly because I knew that in an hour or less I'd be hanging upside down or doing back flips. My stomach often wasn't ready for that *and* food so early in the day.

Most mornings, though, I'd eat a scrambled egg, or some other lean protein that was light and quick. Then I'd put my leotard on under workout clothes and head to a local public high school to run two miles on their track. Once I got to the gym, I'd do about an hour of strength training or other warm ups. Strength training for me consisted of climbing ropes, press handstands, squat jumps, pushups, and pull-ups. I never lifted weights, as they had always intimidated me. Instead, I'd use my own body weight while I did exercises.

Any time I could find a way to get in an extra cardio workout or take a few minutes to stretch, I did. Later on I found Pilates, and that helped my long, lean body become stronger, too. When I describe my body as long, it is important to know that as an adult I am only five-foot-three. But in a gymnast's world, that is pretty tall. I was always the tallest person on my team, and often the leanest.

My height provided me some of my biggest challenges. Many top women gymnasts matured to be less than five feet tall, and the skills I had to master within the sport were designed for people who were shorter and stockier than I was. That meant that even though I had the advantages of having my dad for a coach and two elite gymnasts for parents, I had to work twice as hard as most of the other girls, girls who were shorter and who had more strength and muscle mass. Sometimes it was frustrating to see another girl learn a skill so much more easily than I did. It was as if her body knew exactly what to do, while mine had to practice the skill again and again. I never gave up, though. Whatever it was that I needed to learn, I practiced until it was second nature.

In my daily schedule, training for individual events came after weight training. I worked on bar and beam routines in both my morning and afternoon sessions at the gym, and in the morning also worked on putting individual skills together into routines.

A little before noon, those of us who went to Spring Creek Academy carpooled to school. A few of the kids were home schooled and went their separate ways before we reconnected later in the day. Once at school we'd pack five subjects into two and a half hours with no break, so I usually ate lunch in the car on the way. My mom always packed me a lunch and it typically was a salad with grilled chicken, or fish with rice and vegetables, along with fresh carrots and fruit.

Once in a while, if there was not time to eat on the short drive to school, I ate during my first class, or sometimes in the hall as I walked between classes. Our teachers did not mind, as long as we still paid attention and participated. Every thirty minutes we'd hustle to a new class. I liked the fact that there was no small talk at the beginning of the class, or during it. Each lesson was focused and tightly packed with information. We got in, got it done, and got out, and all of my testing showed that I was staying at or above grade level.

It turned out that I was just as much an over-achiever at school as I was in the gym. I guess I am definitely a perfectionist. Each year we also had to take a standardized grade level test called the Iowa test, and my straight A grades ensured that I did very well on those tests.

One day, however, both my parents picked me up from school. This was an odd occurrence, since I usually carpooled back to the gym with my friends. Maybe I had an appointment, or we were going somewhere together. Whatever the reason, my parents could tell right away that something was wrong, and after a few minutes they wheedled it out of me. I started to cry when I told them I had gotten my report card and had received a grade of 89 in a science class. An 89 was a B. I was so upset, as my goal had been to be a straight A student.

It seems a trivial thing now, but I so wanted to please my parents that I thought they would be disappointed in me, or even worse, mad at me, if I got a B. Of course they were not mad or disappointed. They knew I had done my best, but I resolved to work harder in that class the next semester and I did. The grade of 89 was a good motivator for me to do more, and I did.

I also learned something important from that experience and it was that doing my very best was all I could do. If I gave something my all and I got a B, or even a C, then I could look back on my effort with pride. If, however, I got a B or a C because I had chosen to watch television rather than study, then I lost the opportunity to be proud of myself.

Grades and education were important to me because even though I had not yet considered life after gymnastics, I knew that it was out there somewhere in my murky and distant future. Whatever was in store for me, I knew that I would need a good education.

If my parents did not pick me up from school, at three o'clock we all carpooled back to the gym, and a power bar and some water got me through until dinner. I have also always consumed a lot of water. It is important for everyone to stay hydrated, but especially those who move their bodies a lot, people who do a lot of physical work, such as athletes. Afternoon training consisted of skills, tumbling, and vaulting, and then I was home for dinner and homework.

Even as an older teen I was always in bed by nine or ten PM. If I hadn't finished my homework by that time, well, I'd just train half an hour less the next day. Sleep was that important and the threat of spending even thirty minutes less time in the gym was a huge motivating factor for me to hit the books with a focused mind to get the work done.

I mention this because to achieve success in anything, it takes sacrifice. I sacrificed afternoons at the mall, Friday night movies with friends, sleepovers, other friends' birthday parties, and so much more. Yes, I sacrificed experiencing all of those things but it wasn't a sacrifice for me at all. I chose to focus on my sport. I chose to do as well as I could in school, and train as much as I could. Besides, I was having fun and could not imagine living my life any other way. Whatever your goal is, you have to carve out the time to make it happen, then actually be focused and productive during the time you spend working on it.

An extra incentive for me was seeing my dad's four Olympic medals. He kept them in a box in the basement, and the first time I pulled them out of the box, I was so amazed. I was actually in awe. I had far too much respect for my dad, the medals, and what the medals represented to ever put them on. But, as far back as I can remember I knew how cool it was to be a world-class gymnast like my parents, and I always wanted to be just like them.

I don't remember when I put two and two together and understood that my mom was a world champion gymnast, and my dad was an Olympic gold medalist. I don't even remember when I first began to understand what the Olympics were, but I must have been fairly young. All I knew was that when it came to my dad's Olympic success, I wanted similar medals for my own. Always, I wanted to be just like my dad.

Fridays and Saturdays we only trained in the morning, and we rested on Sundays. I often chose to swim or spend time with friends on Sunday afternoons. That way I got to do everything other girls my age did, just not as much or as often, since I limited my out-of-gym social time to short periods on the weekends. Closer to big competitions, I'd do fewer things with my friends, and use the time for extra rest. However, that was my choice. Always, it was what I chose to do and I can say that I do not regret any of those choices.

We also had dogs around our house when I was growing up, and they were a constant source of joy. Layla was a brown and white Springer spaniel that we got when I was three or four from our wonderful family friend, Pat Hamilton. Layla was as much a part of our household as any of the rest of us. As I grew up, I poured out my joys, challenges, and sorrows to her, and she always gave me whatever I needed. Attentive listener? Absolutely. Doggie kisses? Check. As an only child, I needed her in my life so very much.

I needed human friends, too, and had several who were very close. My best friend during this time was a gymnast named Nina Kim. Nina remains one of my best friends to this day, but when we first met she had moved from Houston to Dallas to train with my parents. I must have been about ten at the time. Her family had to stay in Houston so she lived with the family of one of my team-mates. I thought of my dad being away from his family and knew how hard that was for him. It must have been hard for Nina, too.

My new friend was several years older than I was, but that wasn't a problem for me. Most of my close friends were a little older. I wasn't sure if that was a sign that I was more mature than my actual years, or a reflection back to my early years of yearning to be just like the "big girls." In any case, Nina and I understood each other completely. We connected from the very start and she was the one I laughed and giggled with, and told my secrets to.

One of the true signs of friendship is loyalty, and Nina stuck by my side even when things weren't going my way. You might not think it, but I had a good number of those days, days when I left the gym discouraged and disappointed in myself. When I struggled with a new skill or had trouble with an injury, Nina was the one who encouraged me and helped me keep in sight my end goal of becoming an Olympic champion. And, I did the same for her. Through Nina and many of the other people I became close to, I learned that friends do not all have to have the same goals, or even the same interests. They just have to respect and care for each other, and listen when someone needs to talk things through.

The one day of the year when I got to see all of my friends was my birthday. I always had my parties at the gym and I remember, particularly when I was very young, bouncing on the trampoline and tumbling over and over across the floor mats with my friends. And, because I was born on October 30, the day before Halloween, I invited all of my friends to arrive in costume. Each year I'd dress up as a different character. Dressing up as Dorothy from the *Wizard of Oz* is among one of my favorite Halloweens memories, although I had other costumes as well. A bunny, a pumpkin, and an angel come to mind, as does a cow costume on a really cold Halloween. I was a very bundled-up little cow.

For my gymnast friends, my birthday was a time where we could relax and have fun, and for those non-gymnast friends from school, it was a time where they could see where I spent most of my out of school hours. I am very glad that my parents were athletes who taught me how to eat properly, but sometimes an extra helping of birthday cake is just the thing that is needed to help a little girl turn another year older.

I can now see how important those early years were for me. I developed a good work ethic, learned how to get to know all different kinds of people, discovered healthy eating habits, and found a love of learning. Those are all things that will carry me forward throughout my lifetime.

It is never too late to develop a good habit, though, and I am constantly trying to improve myself. For the most part I've found that all it takes is commitment and a conscious effort. I do that by breaking every goal into steps. If I want, for example, to improve my grade in a certain class, I might read through previous chapters in my textbook or look through old homework, decide to spend an extra half hour each day studying, ask my teacher or professor for help or ideas, and make a list of all areas I am not 100 percent clear about. This process has helped me through almost anything I want to achieve.

Not everyone has the advantage of loving friends or a supportive family, but that does not mean you cannot achieve all you ever wanted. Each person has a unique set of challenges. Some are physical challenges, others are emotional, while yet other problems are situational or financial. But just like walking down the road, if you take one step a day toward your goal, eventually you will get there, just as I did.

Chapter Five

While my parents were getting WOGA established, and while I was busy training, our little family had also settled into regular American life. My mom and dad tried to create a mix of what they had grown up with in Russia, along with the usual traditions that Americans followed. I think they did a pretty good job.

For example, Thanksgiving is a big holiday here in the United States, but it is an entirely American holiday, so it is not celebrated in Russia. At all. It must have been hard for my mom and dad to embrace this special day without having grown up with a sense of American history and everything that Thanksgiving embraces. But they tried, and we have always celebrated it.

My parents also grew up during a time in Russia when it was illegal to practice religion of any sort, so they had not known any elaborate Christmas celebrations when they were young. They did begin celebrating the holiday after they moved to the United States with a special dinner, but our biggest holiday of the year, has always been New Year's Eve. This is the most celebrated holiday in Russia, and my parents kept that tradition when they moved here.

In Russia, the New Year's holiday is all about family and being together, so my grandparents often came in from Moscow for a long stay over the holiday. Many of our friends came to share this special time with us as well, and that was good, because Russian tradition says that you should spend New Year's Eve with the people you most want to spend the coming year with. I definitely wanted to spend the New Year with my friends and with people I loved.

As a family, we often had gone somewhere where there was snow for Christmas, or at least during the week between Christmas and New Year's. But, by every New Year's Eve we were home and the scent of baking filled the house. I couldn't wait until five o'clock in the evening when everyone started to arrive. My dad grilled chicken and steak and we ate a mix of Russian and American foods. If there were some Greek, French, or Italian dishes thrown in there too, well, they got eaten just as fast as the others.

We have friends from many countries, so at our New Year's Eve parties there could be as many as five languages being spoken at once. It was always a little bit like a United Nations gathering. My dad's former coach from Russia, Edouard Iarov, and his wife, Rita, now lived nearby. He had also coached in France, so he and most of the other people switched from one language to the next while they talked and shared stories of the past year.

The Russian tradition of toasting to each other's good health and fortune was also done many times throughout the night. Anytime someone could think of something to toast, it was done with much good will and cheer. Then finally, at midnight, we rang in the New Year with our loved ones. When I was younger I often didn't make it until midnight, and sometimes fell asleep on the couch with the murmured voices of friends and family surrounding me. It was such a warm, safe, and peaceful way to fall asleep. Someone always woke me a few minutes before midnight, though, and we'd laugh and hug, and give each other our best wishes for the coming year. I have also fallen asleep before midnight a few times in more recent years. A lifetime of early bedtimes is so ingrained in me that it is hard for me to stay awake.

On New Year's morning when I was young, the first thing that I'd do when I woke up was to reach underneath my pillow to search for the traditional Russian gift that is left there. It was always a small gift, but one that was cherished all the same. It was one of the best times of the year for me—and still is. I am sure there are many more customs and cultural traditions that my parents left behind in Russia, but they wanted to fully adopt their new country, and they wanted me to be an American girl. I am glad, though, that I got to experience at least some of the things my mom and dad did when they were young.

I also made sure that I trained on holidays. A human body does not know anything about celebrations or special days, and I knew that my body needed the consistency of routine that regular training provided. Often when I took a Sunday off, I wasn't at my best on Monday, or even on Tuesday. It took that long for my body to get up to speed after just one day's rest. So, on Thanksgiving, Christmas, New Year's, and other holiday mornings, I'd choose to be at the gym, working hard and looking forward to spending time with my family and friends later in the day. I loved training on holidays, as I was always filled with a special excitement that made me do just a little better. And each time I improved any part of my performance, or mastered a new skill, it gave me more and more confidence that I would eventually make it to the Olympics.

The achievement of a dream often happens in stages. When I was ten years old, I finally got to go somewhere I had always dreamed of going: The USA National Team Training Center! Although I wasn't on the national team yet, I had been invited based on my promising talent. By this time my dad had taken over all of my training, and he sent them a video of me performing. I knew he had sent the video in, and hoped in the way that only a little girl can that the coaches there would like what they saw. When I was invited to come to the camp I was so excited! I had dreamed that I would be chosen someday, but when I got the news I could barely contain myself.

Martha Karolyi was our team coordinator. She is the wife of Bela Karolyi, the legendary gymnastics coach with the big mustache who defected to the United States in 1981 and sought political asylum. Martha defected with her husband. Together, they had trained some of my idols, girls such as Mary Lou Retton, Nadia Comăneci, and Kerri Strug.

Everyone involved with the training camp met in Huntsville, Texas (near Houston) for three or four days every month. Being part of these training camps was a huge step toward my dream, and each camp became a major motivator for me to work even harder. Girls came in from all over the country with their coaches (no families allowed), and in addition to getting to know other top gymnasts and making friendships that would last, in many cases, a lifetime, I got to see what the other girls were working on. Imagine if you could take a sneak peek at a test paper of the top student in your school. That's what it was like for me. I got to see the "big girls" working on all of their new skills and routines. Everyone needs role models and here I was in the same room with several of mine!

My schedule at the camp was similar to what it was at home, except that we trained an hour less. The biggest difference was that even though the training time was shorter, the intensity was much greater with coaches, other gymnasts, and USA Gymnastics staff watching your training. I definitely wanted to be at my best and give my all at the training camps because when I was twelve, I could earn a spot on the junior team. Everything I did at those camps went toward showing the decision makers that I was worthy of that spot.

Most of the girls also did some form of physical therapy as well, and that was at a higher level than we might receive at home. A lot of the PT was an effort to prevent injuries, but there were always a few girls who were getting over an injury, or who had a chronic weak area in her body.

It wasn't all work and no play, however. All the girls stayed in cabins with bunk beds in each bedroom, so we got to know each other pretty well. I had so much fun at the camps, in fact, that I looked forward to them each and every month. And, because the camps were typically held at the end of each month, I got to celebrate my October 30 birthday there, too. Those celebrations consisted only of a cake and a round of "Happy Birthday," but it was lot of fun and went a long way toward making me fit in.

Any difference when you are ten, eleven, twelve, can make a kid feel like an outsider, and even though I wasn't, I often felt like I was. My parents remedied some of that when I was eleven. Because I was a minor child at the time, I became an American citizen by default when my parents earned their US citizenship.

When we moved here, my mom and dad came to the United States on what is known as a "green card." This is a document that serves as proof that the person is a lawful and permanent resident of the country. It also says the person has been granted immigration benefits, which includes permission to live in and become employed in the United States. After a waiting period of five years, green card holders can apply for citizenship.

In our process of becoming United States citizens, we also were able to retain our Russian citizenship. Some countries allow you to do that, and Russia is one of them. Today I couldn't be more proud to be an American.

As an Olympic gymnast I have had the privilege of representing the United States in many countries around the world. I have traveled to many different areas and have gotten to learn about many faiths and cultures. Many countries are great, but none, in my opinion, is greater than the United States of America. That's why I was so proud to stand on the gold medal podium at the Olympics. Yes, I was proud of my accomplishment, but I was proud of my country, too, and very pleased to have won the gold for America.

I regularly hear people complain about how things are here in the United States, but they have developed no plan for positive change. My parents raised me to take action if I felt strongly about something. If I didn't feel something was fair, I learned to research the situation, develop a plan for positive change, then present it to whoever was in charge. That process works, in theory, for improvements to everything from social injustice to something as simple as yucky lunch menus. Complaining without a plan to fix the problem is never productive. If there is a problem, we all need to find a way to make it better.

Over the years, as happens from time to time with athletes, I had injuries. My first real injury came when I was eleven with a stress fracture in my back. I have always been very flexible and the constant bending and twisting eventually took a toll on my backbones. In addition to me being upset that I had to severely limit my training while the injury healed, my parents had costs for physical therapy and other rehabs. We were still on a tight budget, but if my parents cut back in other household areas to pay for the extra rehabs, I was not aware of it. All they wanted was for me to focus on school and my training, so I did. That, in itself, was an incredible gift.

My doctor let my parents know that my particular kind of fracture was a common one, especially with active kids my age, and it would not become serious as long as I rested my body. I hated that I had to wear an itchy back brace for three months, and could only take it off to bathe. To make matters worse, I learned that I was done competing for the year. That sad news made me cry more than once. The brace came all the way down over my hips, but after eight weeks or so, my dad cut the lower part of it away, so I could begin stretching my legs. For every day that an athlete does not train, it takes several days to get the muscles back up to speed. For an Olympic hopeful, three months was a long time to be away from training. Ever since the brace first went on my body, I had begged and cried to be allowed to train, and this was my dad's compromise. It was better than nothing.

Other than my injury, about the only thing that ever put a damper on my mood during that time of my life was the occasional conversation that I heard in the gym. There was always a lot of discussion between kids before, during, and after training, and the topics were wide and varied. Some kids, however, occasionally criticized my dad. I can't tell you how bad that made me feel. I knew how hard he worked and how much he cared for everyone who walked through the doors of WOGA. I wished with everything I had that they would criticize me instead.

Most of the chatter was normal griping, and mostly from kids who didn't want to do the work they needed to do to succeed. I'm not sure if the kids knew I overheard, or if they specifically saved the conversation until I was within earshot. It doesn't matter either way, the words still made me sad and angry. I swallowed my feelings, however, as I didn't want to get caught up in the negativity of those kinds of words, or that way of thinking.

My next few years were big ones for me. In addition to my back injury, I had a huge growth spurt. All of a sudden my arms and legs were much longer and I didn't know what to do with them half the time. I was very self-conscious about my new awkwardness, and it made me feel even more of an outsider than I already felt. Even though being in gymnastics helped me tremendously in coordinating my new lengthy limbs, I was living in a very small public spotlight, and felt there was nowhere to hide.

Within the gymnastics world, it was hard to hear people talk about and criticize my body. I'd also read things about me in magazines about the sport. Depending on whom you listened to I was too thin, too tall, too blond, too . . . something. It wasn't the most inspiring time for a young girl.

What I was experiencing with my body was what every preteen and teen goes through. Still, with my parents who spoke accented English, my Russian birth, and my early successes in gymnastics, I knew I was not "just like" everyone else. How I longed to fit in. Like many kids my age, I thought I was the only one in the world who felt this way.

It took me many years to understand that every young person goes through growth spurts and feels awkward. And while every child did not have the specific set of circumstances that made me feel different, everyone has something that makes them feel set apart. If you don't look exactly like other kids, wear the same clothing brands, have the same haircut, play the same sports, celebrate the same holidays, get the same grades, have the same interests, well, then you are bound to feel different.

I wish, however, that I had understood that every girl I knew, even the older, more together girls, had felt this way at some point in her life. No one is expected to be perfect, and while we might revel in perfect moments or perfect performances, those are just little blips on our big screen of life. Most of the time we struggle to fit in with the many groups that are important to us. School, work, church, family, friends, or sports, there is bound to be one or more areas where you feel you do not fit in, where you want to pull a bag over your head or hide in the corner.

Instead, wouldn't it be great if we could all shine in all our uniqueness? Middle school aged kids can be brutal, though, and now that I am past that age I can see that those kids who called me names, and who made me feel uncomfortable, were probably feeling even more awkward than I was. This acting out toward someone else was just his or her way of dealing with it.

The other thing I learned much later that I wish I had known then was that it was okay if I felt awkward, but it was not okay for me to allow someone else to make me feel uncomfortable, embarrassed, or self-conscious. I had not yet learned my own self-worth, which is something we all already have. That realization would come a few years down the road. In the meantime, I spent quite a bit of time feeling like I was the only little girl in the world who was different. I also didn't yet know that this feeling would eventually lessen, and I wouldn't always feel this way on a daily basis.

When I earned a place on the junior national team when I was twelve, it went a long way toward making me feel good about myself. Hard work and accomplishment, I've learned, have a way of doing that.

Chapter Six

My first national championships were held in 2002 in Cleveland, Ohio, and in my first event, the uneven bars, I went through my warm-ups as usual. When it was my turn to compete, I took a deep breath and went for my routine, as I had done hundreds of times in the gym. It started out well, but then I missed my Gienger release move and fell to the floor as my dad caught me in his arms.

To say I was devastated, well, that would have been an understatement on how I felt. If I could have looked into the future, I would have seen that this was not the only fall that I would have from the bars during a competition. There was another, far more important fall, in my future. But on this day, even though I was not able to finish my routine, I continued on to the rest of the two-day competition and did well enough to make my first junior national team.

A few months later I was thrilled to travel to the Dominican Republic (my first career-based international trip) for the Pan American Championships as part of the national team. But before I left Texas, a huge box had been delivered to me. When I opened it, I found the box contained all of the official USA national team apparel that I would need for the competition—and then some. I spent several exhilarating hours trying on the clothes, and modeling them for my parents. These clothes had special meaning, because you could not just go out and buy them. You had to earn them and they validated my many long hours of training. I still think of them as the best clothes I have ever gotten.

When I was growing up, I had traveled overseas a number of times to visit my family in Russia, so I was an experienced international traveler. But this trip was special; my teammates and I had so much fun. I knew each girl from the monthly training camps we attended, but there was something special about traveling together and the unique experiences we shared that bonded us even more closely. The competition in the Dominican Republic went well, and I earned a gold in the team competition along with my teammates, then I won silver medals in the all-around, bars, and beam.

As I moved into my mid-teens, my body kept changing and I knew I had to keep up nutritionally, so I upped my game on that front. We did not have a nutritionist at WOGA, but my mom has a great analogy, which I understood right away. "You need to treat your body like an expensive car," she said over and over, "and only put the best fuel into it."

The reality is, we are what we eat. Junk in, junk out. That means you will have a harder time concentrating, and a harder time reaching your goals if you eat an unbalanced diet—or food that has a lot of preservatives, dyes, and artificial sugars. Becoming an Olympic medalist was going to be hard enough. I wanted to take every advantage I could, and that included what I ate.

My new commitment to an even healthier diet than I ate before helped me to win a number of competitions in 2003 and 2004 including two junior national all-around titles.

Going into my first year of senior competition in 2005, there was a lot of expectation. Not my expectations of the competitive experience, but in other's expectations of me. I had dominated the USA junior level for the past two years and that put a lot of pressure on me when I finally moved up to compete with the "big girls."

If I had been born just a few months earlier, I could have maybe competed in the 2004 Olympics. But, while that was not to be for me, it was a reality for WOGA. Yevgeny coached a talented gymnast and one of my great friends, Carly Patterson, who became the first American woman to win the gold in the all-around in the twenty years since Mary Lou Retton won it in 1984. In addition, Yevgeny had coached two of the members of the gold medal winning 2003 World Championship team, including Hollie Vise. Carly and Hollie were two of the older girls I had watched for so long and I was beyond excited that they had been so successful. I was also thrilled for Yevgeny and for WOGA. After all, it hadn't been all that long ago when Yevgeny, my parents, and the gym were struggling to survive.

Any athletic sport is as much a mental game as it is a physical one. That is also true of any big event in life: a major test, a job interview, or a move to a new town or state. If your brain is not in the right place, then a lot of things can go wrong. It struck me once again how fortunate I was to have my specific set of parents. They had both been through competitive pressure and could help me direct my thoughts in a positive manner. They, and a continual positive attitude, also helped me with the long four-year wait until the 2008 Olympics.

That strategy worked, as I won my first senior national championship, and then placed second at the world championships in Melbourne. I missed the all-around gold medal there by one one-thousandth of a point. Yes, the scoring was that close. The competition in Melbourne was one of the highlights of my career. It was the first time I felt that I had somewhat made it. It was also the first time that I felt fully accepted by the world press, and by the other athletes and coaches.

Looking back, I am sure that I had been accepted long before then, but that was the first time I felt that I had. Gymnasts peak very early in life. A doctor or lawyer, or even a professional golfer, might not hit their best stride until he or she is, say, forty. A person has a lot more experience in life at that age than they do at sixteen. Unfortunately, I didn't know that then. I was still an awkward teenager inside, but the success of the Melbourne competition and that close second-place finish, gave me a lot of motivation to do even better.

During this time I was still 100 percent focused on my goals. Actually, that's not quite true, I was 1000 percent focused. Nina and I and my other friends had fun with get-togethers, movies and visits to the mall, but never during a time when I normally would be training.

Some of my school friends got their driver's license as soon as they turned sixteen, but I was not tempted. There was no place I wanted to go other than to the gym, school, and home. In fact, I was eighteen before I became motivated enough in that direction and actually took the test for my license. Until then, I had bigger fish to fry.

Dating was another issue that many of my friends were beginning to be interested in, but not me. Oh, there were certain boys whom I liked, but I didn't like them enough to jeopardize a competition or my time at the gym. Between getting a driver's license and becoming interested in boys, several girls I trained with eventually dropped out of the sport. But, if that's where their new interests lay, then that was the right choice for them. It is never productive to force an intense interest in something, such as competitive sports, when the interest simply is not there.

In addition, because my parents had been busy with their own competitive careers when they were my age, they did not have much experience in teen dating, so there was little motherly or fatherly advice on that front. I am also sure that between dating in the Soviet Union in the 1980s and dating in the United States twenty years later there were many social and cultural differences, so any experience my parents might have had probably would not have been of help to me. It is just as well that I was not interested.

I did not want any boy to get between my competitions and me. I didn't realize then, however, that a good, solid relationship with the right person will add to your focus, rather than take away. The right person can motivate and support you. But when I was in my teens, I was not mature enough to understand that. I just saw dating as a distraction that I did not want or need.

One thing I did know, however, was that when I did start to date, I would be looking for my husband. My parents married very young and had me early in their marriage. They are still together today, still very much in love, and I absolutely wanted something just like that. Plus, I didn't see the value in dating several boys at one time, or in seeing people who I wasn't all that interested in. I wanted a deep and personal relationship with a fun, caring, responsible guy. How was I going to find him if I was busy dating people I knew would not be right for me?

I saw a number of girls my age and older make big mistakes with the boys they dated, and I did not want to go through the heartbreak that they experienced. Many of those girls chose poorly, and latched on to the first guy who paid them any attention. My dad and a number of the other male coaches I knew had shown me by example that there were many good, decent guys in the world who would treat his partner with honesty and respect. That's exactly what I wanted, but I was in no hurry to find him. I knew he was out there somewhere, and I could wait.

In my teens, my parents still let me know on a regular basis that I could stop training any time I wanted. But I didn't want that. I still wanted to train all day, every day. Well, the majority of the time that was how I felt. Accomplishing anything worthwhile can be hard work, and training was no different. Some days I'd come home after a bad day in the gym, or even a series of bad days. Then the negative self-talk would start up in my head and I'd bring up the idea of quitting.

My mom is so wise. She'd always hear me out, and then come back with something to the effect of, "You can quit any time you want, but you can't quit after a bad day. When you quit, quit after a good day." That was such great advice and I have found that it works in just about any situation—except really bad relationships. It is not wise or safe to stay in a bad relationship, one where you might become hurt physically or emotionally.

When I was in my teens I never thought past the 2008 Olympics, past the competition, past Beijing. For me, there was no life beyond that. None. It's scary to look back at that now, as most of my friends had some idea what they wanted to do after they graduated from high school, or after the Olympics. Not me. I didn't want to take any of my attention away from my goal. And besides, I was having such a good time getting there that I wanted to fully experience the journey.

Many things can go wrong on the road to a dream, and in the summer of 2006, two short years before the Olympics, I suffered a bad injury to my ankle—a week before the world championships. It was a silly injury, but one that had real consequences. I was jumping on the trampoline in the gym when I rolled my ankle and injured it. I knew immediately that the injury was bad. Not only did it hurt terribly, within minutes my ankle swelled so badly it looked as if a tennis ball was inside of it.

As soon as I realized what had happened, my stomach seemed to drop out of my body, as it does whenever you have a bad shock. It was a horrible realization that I can't equate to anything similar. Maybe if you were being interviewed on national television and all of a sudden you realized you had your pajamas on. That's the kind of sickening feeling that enveloped my entire body.

I won the national championships, and had my eye on a win at the world championships. Then, less than a month later, I hurt my ankle. Now even my Olympic future had been put in jeopardy, and everything I had worked for my entire life was up in the air. In addition to feeling that I'd let my parents down by becoming injured, I also felt that I had let my team and my country down. It was scary not knowing the extent of my injury or what the prognosis was. Could I recover, or was my time with gymnastics at an end?

It turned out that the injury had caused a bone chip near my Achilles tendon. I needed surgery, but the bone chip was not in a critical place and the surgery did not have to be done immediately. After a lot of discussion amongst my doctors, parents, and the staff at USA Gymnastics, we felt I could compete on the uneven bars at the world championships, and that if my ankle was heavily taped the only problem might be the landing at the end of my routine.

I jumped at the chance to compete. The uneven bars usually were my best event. If I could help out my team by delivering a good score, I definitely wanted to do that. Fortunately, I did well, and helped my team win the silver medal. I also earned a silver medal individually in the uneven bar finals, even after taking a step after landing. Ouch, that landing really did hurt.

After the world championships I had the surgery. That was a difficult time for me. Before the injury I had been at the top of my game internationally, and this setback meant I would have a much harder climb getting ready for the Olympics. It was hard to stay positive, hard to sit on the sidelines when I wanted to be training full speed ahead. Well, I never actually sat on the sidelines, as I always did some kind of strength training or stretching, and I also kept some of my skills up on the bars, but I wasn't training nearly as hard as I would have liked.

Eventually my ankle healed well enough for me to resume training at a level I was comfortable with. I was maybe a little impatient with my rehab, however. Not too long after I started back I tweaked my ankle. Not badly, but enough to set me back again.

By this time, a great many people had attached their hopes and dreams for an Olympic win to me. My parents, grandparents, and great-grandparents; all the people at the gym, my friends, their parents, and the coaches; people I went to school with, and seemingly the entire state of Texas. That was just for starters. If I couldn't compete, if my ankle was not strong enough for me to get through the qualifying competitions, I'd disappoint everyone. That was the last thing I wanted to do.

So, I waited, rested, and tried again. That entire year seemed as if I took two steps forward and one step back. My ankle gave way several times that year and each time I wondered if I would ever reach my goal. I was so close to the Olympics and instead of being at my best, I was at my absolute worst.

This was one time in my life where it was very hard to keep focused and stay positive. In the back of my mind I must have known that the possibility existed that I would not get to the Olympics after all, but I would not acknowledge that idea. At all. Other people were probably thinking that all of my hopes and dreams were going to be washed away by one silly turn of my ankle. I, however, refused to let that thought into the forefront of my mind.

One benefit of the injury was that I had time to think, plan, and visualize my way back to competitive status. In my mind, I reminded myself that I would not fail. I told myself over and over that my ankle was going to heal up perfectly, and that I was definitely going to the Olympics. During this difficult time I also learned that impatience does not get you anywhere. Good things come to those who work hard, but good things also come in their own time frame. I could do all the rehab, all the stretching, and have the best diet in the world, but my ankle was still going to heal in its own time frame. I could help it along, but I couldn't rush it. That was a big realization.

During that time I also refused to give credit to the members of the press who called me "washed up," or "over." *What are they thinking*, I asked myself. Washed up? No way. I hadn't yet peaked. I knew I hadn't. Instead, every day that I did not train fully, every day that I did not compete, I looked at as one day that I was closer to being ready to go. Someday, someway, somehow, I knew I would get to the Olympics, and I was determined to do well when I got there.

Olympic dreams aside, I had to finish high school and when it came time for my prom, I knew I wanted to go. My mom and dad didn't quite get the prom concept though, as they did not have a prom or an equivalent kind of event when they were growing up in Russia. Even if they had such an event, my parents probably would have been away at a training camp or a competition. They both had been accepted into the sports track at their respective schools, where the scholastic content was focused on the athletic life, rather than on social skills. So, it took a bit of explaining to get them to realize that this was more than the average party. For the prom I needed an awesome dress, and then there was the limo my friends and I wanted to share.

I didn't have a boyfriend, but I had a dear guy friend whom I had trained with for some time. Steve Legendre went to Spring Creek Academy and trained at WOGA with one of our other coaches. He went on to have a great gymnastics career, was an Olympic alternate for the 2012 Games, and hopes to make the 2016 team. Recently he got married, and he and his wife welcomed a baby girl not too long ago! In high school, however, we were wonderful friends, as we were going through many of the same school, gymnastics, and life stages at the same time. Steve was considered a "good boy" by my parents, and became my prom date.

At Spring Creek, we had such a small class, just twenty-five students, that our prom was kind of an all-high school prom, rather than a senior prom. It was so much fun to get dressed up. I wore a beautiful salmon colored dress and my friends and I loved arriving at the prom in a big, stretch limo. So many of my classmates were on the brink of exciting things, including me. It was wonderful to connect with my friends in a social event such as this, because we knew we'd all scatter soon to begin the next stages of our lives. Our prom ended earlier than you might think, as most of us had training commitments the next morning, and I was in bed by ten-thirty—a very late bedtime for me!

Not too many days later, in spring of 2007, I became a high school graduate. That was a special moment for me for several reasons. One, I knew that I would not see some of my friends as much after this, and that made me a little bit sad. And two, graduating gave me another enormous sense of accomplishment. I still had no clue what my life would look like after the 2008 Olympics, but I knew that my high school diploma would set me up and give me options for whatever came next.

Because our class was so small we had the graduation ceremony in a building on the campus of the University of Texas–Dallas. Graduation found me in the middle of another Russian/American cultural difference. In Russia, these things are not a big deal, while here in the United States lots of families go to elaborate lengths to host huge graduation parties. Many of the larger schools also have all-night class parties. A few of my friends had parties, but if I went to any of them, I didn't stay long. I loved my friends, but I also wanted to train.

My mom attended my graduation while my dad was beyond happy to know I'd made it through school. I never wanted anything more than to make them proud. And on this day, I knew without a doubt that both my mom and my dad were proud of me. I still get a warm and fuzzy feeling inside when I think of that.

That sense of pride alone was worth every second of every minute that I spent studying, or in school.

Another benefit of finishing high school was that with the Olympics a little more than a year away, I could now train full time in the gym. That was another big reason my parents and I were glad I had finally graduated. Now, my head would not have to be partially focused on schoolwork and my studies, so mentally and physically I could spend the next year gearing up to be at my absolute peak in Beijing in 2008. That was, if I made the team. My ankle injury had made me fully aware that anything could happen between now and then.

Chapter Seven

*A*s 2007 rolled into 2008, and as I became stronger both mentally and physically, I knew I needed an additional goal to succeed at the Olympic trials that were coming up in June. I had loved our dog Layla, so much, but she had lived a good doggie life and had passed away the year before. She left a big hole in our family and I missed her far more than I can express in words. Helping fill the gap were the two Labradors we had by this time: Lexi, who was a yellow lab, and Rex, who was a chocolate lab.

As if we didn't have enough dogs, I desperately wanted a puppy and begged my parents to let me get one if I made the Olympic team. They said sure, of course I could have a puppy. And even though they said it in a way that made me think they'd forget about my request (or think I'd forget about it) I kept the vision of a small, cuddly dog close in my mind throughout the spring and early summer of 2008. We all need motivation and I have learned to take mine wherever I can find it.

At our monthly training camp, tension was rising amongst all the girls. There typically were twenty to thirty girls at camp, but only six could make the Olympic team. It goes without saying that every girl there wanted to be on the team. Oddly enough, however, as the year progressed the tension brought out the best in each of us. Every girl there was giving her all, and as each other

girl stepped up her game, I stepped up mine. Ultimately we all became better, but only time would tell if better was going to be good enough at the Olympics.

Camp is an odd place because all of the girls are friends, but we are also fierce competitors. We pulled together tightly for the team competitions, but it was one girl against the next for individual events. To succeed in the camp environment, it took a delicate balance of friendship and competitiveness, especially as some of us roomed together. I imagine this same balance is also needed in many workplaces, especially in sales departments, so I looked at this, too, as good training for my future, whatever that was going to be.

Each month at camp we had a mini-competition where we had to do one, single routine. The scores we received from the judges were then used to rank us according to how well we had performed. The rankings were important to me for several reasons. First it was verification of my status. Good or bad, I knew where I was as compared to other girls. And second, it gave me a direction for my next month's training. I absolutely knew what I had to work on.

Some months at camp I was injured or not feeling well, but I still had to go out there and do my best with some sort of a routine. It didn't matter how sore I was. Other girls were sore, too, but going out there, no matter what, taught me determination, responsibility, and accountability—all good life skills.

These months leading up to the Olympics were some of the happiest of my life. My ankle was getting stronger, I was training well, and I had strong hopes that my lifetime dream would soon come true. I never thought past the Olympics. Never. Looking back at that time in my life, I had no idea who I would be without gymnastics, or without my routine of training and competing. We all have a sense of self, of who we are inside. In 2008, and indeed most of my life, I was the blond, Russian-born American gymnast. I thought of myself as someone who was friendly and

loyal, a person who loved her family, her country, and her dogs, but beyond that, I had no idea. What would I be? Who would I become? What did I want to do? I had to put all of those thoughts aside, because if I let them, they could consume me. Besides, it was much easier for me, and much more fun, to focus on my training.

Early in 2008 I also created a vision board, complete with images of Olympic medals and the Eiffel Tower (I'd always wanted to go to Paris). Also on the board were pictures or reminders of smaller goals I wanted to achieve. Many of these goals were skill based, but I needed to focus on them if I were to achieve them. I put the board on the bench of the window seat in my room and looked at it every day. My mom also hung one of my dad's gold medals on the corner of the board. Now that was inspiring! I can't tell you how much I wanted one of those for my own.

My vision board was a big source of motivation for me. For some people motivation can come in the form of seeing a friend or family member achieve something wonderful. Others find it in books or movies or music, or in the words of people they love. Just seeing the photos (and that medal) on my vision board kept me focused, grounded, and on track. And, it was a great feeling when I could swap out the photo of a goal I had just reached for an image of a goal that was brand new.

As I got closer to the Olympic Trials in Philadelphia in June of 2008 I stopped reading, listening to, or watching any coverage of the sport of gymnastics or the upcoming Olympics. This was a policy my dad had put into place long ago, and was implemented several weeks before any of his athletes got to a big event. It was a very good idea, because otherwise I might have come to believe part of the hype that surrounded some of the other gymnasts, or become discouraged at what reporters might have said about me.

It is always hard not to care what others think or say about you. But my dad's plan for me was for us to all believe that my goal was possible, and my family and I did not want to get distracted by what other people might think. We knew that the only opinions that counted were our own. We believed I could do this, so the television and all other forms of media stayed turned to the off position.

When I got to Philadelphia, I knew that everything I had worked on for so many years hung on the next few days. I was at the top of my field in most of my events, but I knew that one fall, one missed skill, could keep me from my dream. We had a very strong team that year, and a number of girls were vying for a very few slots.

I took each event one at a time, rather than trying to think of all of the routines I would have to get through: vault, bars, beam, and floor. Over the years I'd found that by biting off small chunks of a big goal, it became less intimidating and far more doable. One thing at a time.

Focus, determination, practice, and the support of my friends and family lifted me up, and when all was said and done, I had placed second overall behind Shawn Johnson, who was another rising star in our world. I was going to the Olympics! On one hand, I almost couldn't believe it, but on the other, my goal of reaching the Olympics had become so ingrained into the core of my being that I could not have envisioned any other outcome. If I had missed this opportunity to go to Beijing, I am pretty sure that I would have dug in and worked even harder toward 2012, but I am just as glad that I will never know how I might have reacted, or what I would have done.

I thought that being an Olympic athlete would make me feel different, would change me in some profound way. But it didn't. I was still Nastia. I was still the gymnast who sometimes felt that she didn't fit in. But was I happy? Oh, yes! I was totally, completely, absolutely on top of the world.

As soon as I knew I had made the team I reminded my mom and dad about the puppy. They might have forgotten about it, but they made good on their promise and soon I was cuddling little Ella, a warm and loving black toy poodle. She was, and is, a joy, and has become a welcome addition to our family. My parents think the world of her, and even as small as she was, she fit in well with our existing four-legged friends.

The next six weeks were a flurry of activity, and I spent most of my time perfecting my routines and bringing my body to peak shape through diet, training, rest, physical therapy, massage, acupuncture, and every other method that we could think of. In August, in San Jose with my teammates just before we left for Beijing, I received my box of official USA Olympic team wear. Talk about exciting!

My dad and I flew to Beijing with the team a few weeks before the Olympics. Then, a few days before the competition started, my mom and Nina Kim flew over. They stayed in a hotel in town. My dad stayed with other coaches, and I got to stay in the Olympic Village. Our team had an apartment in a building that housed all of the USA athletes. Each floor of the building housed a different sport (or sometimes several sports), but all members of the gymnastics team were on the same floor.

Our apartment had three bedrooms and we bunked two to a room in twin beds. My roommate happened to be my teammate, Shawn Johnson. We also had two bathrooms in our apartment, a small living room, and a small television so we could watch the various competitions as they took place.

Downstairs, the physical and massage therapists had set up, and there was a common area where all of the USA athletes could hang out. When we weren't training, which it seemed we did all the time, our team hung out in the common area. It was a great place to get to know each other. And then there was the cafeteria that all of the Olympians ate in. It was enormous, and seemed as big as a football field. It was open twenty-four hours a day, and had many choices of food from around the world. Coaches and athletes were the only ones allowed to eat there, but it was still crowded most of the day and night. There were also a lot of languages being spoken all at once, but that made it feel like home.

We also often bumped into athletes from other countries when we were going to our training building or the cafeteria, or waiting for the bus that took us to various locations around the village or to the many sports venues that were part of the Games.

I remember meeting Dirk Nowitzki, a German basketball player who at that time was also playing with the Dallas Mavericks. Here, however, he was playing for the German basketball team. I was a huge Mavericks fan and Dirk was by far my favorite player. I hate to admit that I fell all over myself when I met him, but I did. I was officially star-struck!

I was about five-foot-two during the 2008 Olympic Games and Dirk is seven feet tall. When I got close to him, I could see that I didn't even come up to his chest. I got all giddy when he looked down at me, but I managed to tell him that I was from Dallas, too, and that I was his biggest fan. He was kind enough to pose for a picture with me, and afterward, my teammates teased me mercilessly. It was all in good fun, though, and I am still glad that I made the effort to meet someone I so admired.

Today, when people come up to me and become flustered at meeting me, I wish I could tell them how well I can relate. The reality is that Dirk and I—and any other celebrity or person you might meet—are just people. We have strengths and weaknesses in our abilities and personalities, just as everyone else does. We are not perfect, no one is. I am one who loves to meet people and get to know them, but someone else might not feel that way. Sometimes, though, I'm caught off guard when a fan approaches. I might be running late to a meeting when I am stopped, or have to jump on a scheduled phone call. I never want to give the impression that I am impatient, but sometimes the timing is not good and I have to hurry through a photo or an autograph with a fan. Always, I wish that I had more time to talk. I am so glad, though, that I got to meet Dirk, and that he graciously took the time to meet a young fan.

Travel around the village and various complexes could be slow. There were thousands of people who had to be moved to a lot of different places, and there were a number of different bus routes. We made sure to leave the apartment long before we needed to be somewhere, as the wait time for a bus could be half an hour, or longer. And, we always checked that we were getting on the right bus. We certainly didn't want to end up on a cross-country course or the kayak river.

Because coaches had access to the Olympic Village, I saw my dad all the time. We always ate and rode the bus together, and of course, we spent many hours in training. I could not see my mom or Nina until all of my competitions were over, though, and that was hard. Thanks to modern technology however, we were able to text and call each other regularly, and my mom gave my dad little notes to give to me. They were simple notes, but they meant the world: I LOVE YOU. GOOD LUCK TODAY. I MISS YOU.

It doesn't take much to tell someone how much you care, and those notes kept my mom's love for me in the front of my mind. I carried them with me throughout each day and they gave me a nice feeling inside. I often think that we do not let our loved ones know often enough how we feel. It is often assumed that a specific couple loves each other, for example, but the words are rarely spoken. Just as the bullying words of my youth took me down, other words build me up. These words, from a mom I love so much, were precious.

Other words were also directed at me, but I am so glad that I never heard them. My dad watched over me before the competition to keep me as far away from the media as he could. It wasn't always possible to keep me entirely secluded from reporters, but he did the best he could. In one instance I did not know about until much later, a reporter was, to put it kindly, trashing me at a pre-Games press conference. "How can you think she is a serious contender?" was just one of the questions the reporter asked my dad in a badgering tone.

The questions and the comments became even harsher, until my dad lashed out at the reporter and reminded that woman and the rest of the press of their responsibility as journalists and as adults. Who were these people, my dad asked, to verbally tear down the life-long dream of an athlete, especially a teenaged one? Whatever happened to reporting the facts, reporting the hopes and dreams of each competitor, and telling Olympic fans about the long and challenging road each athlete had traveled? Why do you reporters, he said, have to put the idea in everyone's mind that an athlete has no chance? How do you know that? Anything can happen here at the Olympics.

I am so grateful that I never heard these hateful words from members of the press at the time when they were spoken, although I really would have liked to have seen my dad take them on. Certainly, there was enough pressure on me and every other Olympian there without the negative bashing of some inconsiderate reporters.

How the 2008 Olympics went for me is public record, and maybe is one reason you picked up this book in the first place. In addition to winning the gold in the all-around, I helped my team earn a silver medal, and I earned individual silver medals on the beam and bars, and a bronze on floor. The team competition was held before the individual event finals and I was beyond thrilled with the team silver medal draped around my neck. I remember going back to the Team USA building in the village, feeling like I was floating on air, when I bumped into swimmer Michael Phelps. Here I was with my one medal, and by that time he had already earned eight—all gold, by the way. That put it all into perspective for me, but I still felt like I was floating.

After winning the all-around I was so incredibly happy. The next morning both of my parents and I, and Shawn Johnson (who won the silver) and her parents were interviewed on the *Today* show. That was one of many, *many* interviews that I did post-Olympics. My win was of special interest to the media because I was only the third American woman in the history of the Olympics to win the all-around. I was so proud to join Mary Lou Retton and fellow WOGA gymnast Carly Patterson in achieving this special honor.

Plus, it was only the fourth time in the history of the Olympics that the gold and silver medals had gone to women gymnasts from the same country. Shawn and I joined a pair of Romanian gymnasts who took gold and silver in 2000, and two sets of Soviet gymnasts who accomplished the same feat in 1952 and 1960. Finally, with my five medals, I had tied the Olympic record for the most medals won by an American gymnast in a single Games. The other gymnasts who had also earned this honor were Mary Lou Retton and Shannon Miller.

My purse was a little bit heavier when I headed home, but the reality of what had just been accomplished had not yet sunk in. That did not happen until I got off the plane in Dallas to find thousands of people waiting for me and cheering. To see that so many people cared brought me to tears. Many of the people I didn't even know; they just wanted to come out to congratulate me and welcome me home.

I still get emotional when I think about it, and my homecoming is one of those special moments that I will hold close and treasure forever. It was one thing to know I had fans, but it was another to see so many of them right there. I really appreciated each person who came out. Everyone has busy lives and the fact that these people took time out of theirs to come see me still makes me so grateful.

I was also thrilled that I no longer had to long for my dad's Olympic medals, as I now had some of my own. It became a running joke between my dad and me that I had five medals and he only had four. But he'd come right back with the fact that he had two gold medals and I only had one. Whenever we have that playful discussion, I just smile inside.

When I finally got home, I went to my room and looked at my vision board with new eyes. Mine were now the eyes of an Olympic all-around gold medalist gymnast. I still could hardly believe it. Then I looked more closely. In addition to my dad's medal, there was a new card on my vision board, a card my mom had put there after my dad and I left for Beijing, but before she had left. On the front of the card, in big, blue letters was the word "bravo." Inside, the card read: DEAR NASTIA, CONGRATULATIONS FROM SOMEONE WHO HAS ALWAYS BELIEVED IN YOU. LOVE, MOM.

The level of belief my mom had in me made me cry for the second time that day. She fully believed, really believed with everything she had, that I would win—even before the competition began. Her love for me was endless, and somehow, even though I had not seen the words on the card before, it was as if I had always known they were there.

Chapter Eight

After the Olympics were over, and after I was home, I came to understand that I was not remotely prepared for the barrage of media attention that surrounded me. Again, I thank my lucky stars that I have the mom and the dad that I do, as they helped me stay grounded. They, too, had experienced some media attention after their successes, but not nearly to this extent. First, there were not as many members of the media in Russia as there are here in the United States, and second, there was not as much media, period, in 1988 as there was in 2008. Both cable television and the Internet had blossomed during the last twenty years, and boy what a difference those two things made.

In addition to the onslaught of interviews came a number of awards. These awards were not related to the Olympics, but were given in recognition of my performance there. Among many other awards, I was named the United States Olympic Committee's Female Athlete of the Month for August 2008, and was the same committee's choice of Sportswoman of the Year. Then the Women's Sports Foundation honored me with the award for Individual Sportswoman of the Year. I was also named Sportswoman of the Year for USA Gymnastics and FIG's (International Gymnastics Federation) Athlete of the Year. This last honor was especially cool, as the FIG is the international governing body over gymnastics. It was founded on July 23, 1881 in Liege, Belgium and is currently the world's oldest existing international sport organization.

I was surprised, honored, and humbled by every honor, and appreciative of every award. Yes, I worked hard, but other athletes worked hard and were successful, too. In a society like ours, a society that tends to be superficial, it might have been easy to expect awards like these to come, or not to be excited about them when they did. But I never expected them, and I was always excited about each one. I am still grateful to the individual committee members who chose me.

Despite all the continued excitement and celebration, I was beginning to feel a post-Olympics letdown, as I felt I had no direction. I'd reached my Olympic goal—and then some—but I wasn't sure what my next goal (or goals) should be. I never wanted to be a person who had reached the highest point in her life when she was eighteen. There were many good, productive, impactful years ahead of me, I knew, and many more successes. I just had no idea what they would be. For the first time in my life I was lost and confused.

Most of my friends were now sophomores in college. They had already set in place a career direction for themselves that would point them down life's winding path. But me? I'd just wake up in the morning and think, *what's next?*

Fortunately I didn't have too long to think, as I was scheduled to go on a post-Olympics tour with Shawn, Shannon Miller, and a number of other male and female gymnasts. Solo music artist Jordan Pruitt and the all-girl band K.S.M. went with us, and performed during our routines. The 2008 tour of USA Gymnastics Superstars hit three-dozen cities between September 7th and November 16th, and we went all across the country.

I have to say, we had a blast. The travel was a lot of fun as I got to see parts of America that I had not yet visited. We have a lot of great cities here and each one taught me something new about this wonderful country. Someday, I hope to go back to many of them to explore more on my own.

The camaraderie between all of the gymnasts was fun, too. Other than the boys who trained at WOGA, and the guys I met at the bigger competitions, I had not had time to really get to know many of our country's male gymnasts. They had a separate monthly training camp that was in Colorado. Their competitions were different than ours, and were often held at different times. They also had a rings competition that we did not have. But now we all got to bond and the boys on the tour became like older brothers to us. I remain thankful to have had this fun opportunity to become friends with so many great and talented gymnasts.

The best part about the tour, though, was that this was the first time I had the chance to interact with gymnastics fans in a meaningful way. Every day I learned over and over again how passionate they were about our sport. I could relate to that! I also learned how much of an inspiration I was to them. Honestly, this was something I had not expected. I took it, though, and vowed to always be the role model they expected me to be. It wasn't hard. I was never one to color outside the lines, so to speak, but I did understand in an entirely new way that if I did something out of character and fell out of the public's good graces, that I would disappoint a lot more people than just my family and me.

Everyday each one of us has the opportunity to influence people around us: friends, family, neighbors, and co-workers. Some of these people are younger and desperately want to fit in, so they behave just like you do. If you are not making a positive mark on the world, then they won't either. It can be an eye-opener to realize that, but it's true. I think of that every day and always try to be encouraging and empowering in the right direction.

On the tour, I also began to hear stories from young girls, some gymnasts and some not, who struggled with body image, self-esteem, bullying, and fitting in, all things I had also struggled with. I decided that someday I'd be in a position to talk more with girls just like these, and be able to talk with them one-on-one. I didn't know when, where, or how, I just knew that it was important enough to me that I had to make it happen. Someday.

After the Olympics and the tour, my parents and I finally took a long-overdue trip to Russia, and when we went the first thing I packed were all of my medals. I wanted to show them to my great-grandparents. I wish I could have captured the emotion in the room when my great-grandfather Boris, the one who years earlier had sent me the drawing of how to hold the bars, took my medals into his hands. Let's just say there were a lot of happy tears, and many of them were mine.

Our older generations are so important. Older people have so much wisdom and experience to share. If we'd only slow down and take the time to listen we'd learn a lot and probably avoid making many of life's mistakes.

While we were in Russia my dad and I also did a few television talk show interviews. Actually, I was quite surprised that these media outlets wanted to talk to me. After all, I had competed for the United States, not Russia. In addition, the Russian women's team had not done well at the Games, so the idea of the interviews felt somewhat uncomfortable to me at first. But, I have to say that I was fully embraced by the media there. Over and over I heard that the Russian people felt that even though I was on the American team, I had won for them, too. And, I reminded myself, even though my Russian language skills were a little rusty, I was still a Russian citizen.

I thought it wonderful that the Russians looked at my success as a unifying achievement, rather than as an event that divided our sport and our countries. They could easily have felt that way, but I believe I was just as loved and embraced by them as I was by American media and fans. It was a nice and pleasant surprise, and one that I treasure.

Now that I had achieved the goal I had worked on my entire life, it was time to spread my wings, and take a few tentative steps toward adulthood. I first put my medals in a safe in my parent's house. I didn't want to take any chance that something would happen to them, and like my dad, I didn't want to make a big show of displaying them. I knew I had earned them, and that was enough. Occasionally I needed the medals for a media appearance or an exhibition, and when that happened, my mom was kind enough to fly with the medals to wherever I was. As good as the overnight delivery services are here in the United States, I did not want to trust any of them with my precious Olympic achievements.

Next, I bought a townhouse. As an Olympic athlete, I was fortunate enough to work with several companies and sponsors who helped support my training. Training at an elite level is like a full-time job, and like everyone else, athletes have to be able to pay their bills. I had a series of wonderful sponsors, companies who supported me with products and/or financially. It is incredibly expensive to achieve an Olympic dream, and the great people at these great companies helped make my dream a reality.

I saw the townhouse as not only a place for me to start my journey into being an adult, but as a sound financial investment. It was located in an up-and-coming area near the gym that was filled with a number of cool new restaurants and shops that were within walking distance. If I ever wanted to move out of the townhouse, I knew I could always rent it out or sell it. All of this was a lot of responsibility, but I felt more than ready for it. Plus, interior design had always been a passion of mine, and I had so much fun decorating my new space.

Once I had moved, I found that for the first in my life I could get up when I wanted, eat what I wanted, stay up as late as I wanted, and do everything else exactly how I wanted. It was wonderful! Being raised by two working parents made me self-sufficient at an early age. Even when I lived at home I had washed my own clothes and did other chores around our house, so I loved digging in a little deeper to become fully responsible for me.

Some of this meant paying utility and other bills associated with living on my own. Light bulb out in the hallway? My responsibility. No food in the refrigerator? My responsibility. It definitely was an adjustment, but one that I loved. Through gymnastics I had learned to be very ordered in my thinking, and that came in handy in stepping up to these new responsibilities.

Now that the gymnastics tour was over I once again found myself at loose ends, and after a brief absence, I began going back to the gym every day. Gymnastics had been such a big part of my life that I wasn't yet ready to let it go. I wasn't training seven hours a day, as I had before, but I was there, training, and working on something every day. I don't think my presence in the gym was a surprise to anyone, including myself. I had such a passion for the sport that I did not feel I was being my best self if I was not practicing it in some way, shape, or form.

My plans for 2009 and beyond were still very fluid. I thought I might compete again, but I also enrolled at Southern Methodist University (SMU). Most of my friends from school were already a year or more ahead of me on the education front, and I wanted to dip my toe into the water to see what was out there.

When I enrolled at SMU, however, my mom and dad shook their heads, saying, "You have too many post-Olympic commitments." I was only taking one psychology and one philosophy class, but starting college was important to me. This is what my friends were doing, and taking classes made me feel normal.

SMU had a beautiful campus along with a strict attendance policy, and due to my extensive travel schedule I soon found that I had missed so many classes that I had to withdraw. I hated that because I liked to finish what I started, but I understood. And, there was a little part of me that hated to admit that my mom and dad had been right. I was glad that my parents let me feel my own way, though, and that even though they had given me their advice; that they had not continued to discourage me.

I resolved that this first attempt at college would not be my last. A good education was critical to lifelong success. The timing was just not right for me at this point in time, but I knew there would be a point in the future when that would change. So with my townhouse, the constant love of my parents, and my daily training at the gym, I felt very safe in my new explorations of life.

Everyone makes his or her own transitions in different ways. I knew enough about myself to go slowly and make gradual changes to my life. I also wanted to do it on my own terms and not have other people or the circumstances life can throw at you make decisions for me. Sometimes, sink or swim, you have to succeed or fail on your own. There are a lot of lessons to be learned in failure. You just have to pick yourself up afterwards, regroup, and go on.

A lot of people think I dropped out of sight for a few years after the Olympics. I didn't, really. I participated in a few competitions, and I had a lot going on in addition to training. Besides my attempt at college, I had a lot of chances to work with different companies, and also with sponsors in one capacity or another.

In September of 2008, just weeks after the Olympics, I was honored by having my photo placed on the front of a box of Wheaties cereal. Over the years General Mills had placed many deserving athletes on the cover of their Wheaties boxes, and I couldn't believe they chose me to be part of this special tradition.

In addition to Wheaties, I was given many other exciting opportunities, including developing my own clothing lines. I had always loved fashion, and had worn GK Elite leotards since I was ten. When I found out we could work together to design my own line, I was ecstatic. You know how you have a favorite pair of jeans or a top that you love—except for that one little thing? Maybe the color was wrong, or the fabric too stretchy. This was my opportunity to put my ideas into play.

I hand drew my designs, and then sent them off to the GK designers for them to tweak. My mom and I sometimes drew them together, as she had also spent a lot of years in a leotard. Not only was this a great way for us to spend time together, it was a way for me to stay connected with the sport.

A few times I flew to the GK offices and met with their designers as we made final decisions on colors and fabrics. Everyone was so kind, and unlike some other celebrity-labeled clothing lines where it is only the celebrity's name on the line, GK took my input seriously. These leotards were truly my ideas come to life.

I was also so fortunate to be able to work with JCPenney and Warner Bros. Consumer Products to develop a fashion collection called Supergirl by Nastia. It was a casual wear line that came in kids' sizes 4-6X, and 7-14. I was so proud the day the line launched because the fashions were cute, fun, and affordable. The line was also about empowerment for girls, which after talking to the fans on the post-Olympic tour, was becoming a passion of mine.

I also helped design a line of bar grips and other gym equipment with AAI and DGS. This, the leotards, and the clothes were all done in the spirit of making young women proud of themselves. From personal experience I know if you feel good in what you wear, you will walk taller and prouder, and project more confidence in yourself—good things all around.

Too many kids, and adults, give up on themselves before they even get started in life. No matter your circumstances, if you work hard you can become whoever you want to be. It takes time, dedication and patience, and often the help of a teacher, boss, neighbor, family member, or friend who believes in you. But, you *can* succeed. It's just a little easier to do if you are wearing clothes that you really, *really* like.

And then there was gymnastics. I made my first post-Olympics competitive appearance at the CoverGirl Classic in July of 2009 in Des Moines, Iowa. This was about eleven months after the Olympics. The decision to compete again was not an easy one for me. I had already achieved my life goal of winning an Olympic medal. In fact, I had won five and earned a gold in the all-around. There was nothing left for me to prove to myself or anyone else, but I just couldn't let it go. I loved gymnastics so much, loved competing, that I knew I wasn't yet done.

This time I only competed on beam. At this point it was too time consuming for me to try to work on all of the events. In this competition I placed second behind another great friend, Ivana Hong, who not only trained at WOGA, but was also coached by my dad. Because of that, my feeling was that we all won. I went with beam again at the United States Championships, placed fourth, and was added to the national team. But even though I also was chosen for the world championships selection camp, I decided to decline the invitation. I knew how tough and competitive the girls would be at world championship level, and also knew I was not fit enough to be competitive with them.

One thing I learned during my competitive career was that it is critical to know your own strengths and weaknesses. Actually, you need to know them better than anyone else does. Are you really ready for a job promotion, to begin graduate school, or a move to a new country? Have you taken all the steps you need to be the best you can be for each of those events? When it came to the world championships, I knew I was not ready. Increased media attention, balancing my new adult life, college, and the clothing and equipment lines had taken away from time I needed to have spent in the gym to bring myself to world competition level. So I pulled out. It was my decision and it was the right decision for me.

Whenever I make a decision like that I weigh all the plusses and minuses, and also get input from my family and closest friends. I am not one to make a big decision lightly, or without first gathering all the information I can find. Only then do I make the best decision for me, one that will set me up for the best success possible.

Unfortunately, many people criticized me for my decision, but I had finally come to terms with negativity like that. Those people knew nothing about me and I had learned to only let the opinions of people who love and cherish me affect me. Those negative people would also have criticized me if I had competed, and done poorly because I hadn't been ready. With some people, you never can win.

Chapter Nine

By the end of 2011, I had decided to try for another Olympics. Back in 2008, I had felt one way or another that I would be in London in 2012, and this was the familiar way for me to get there. But as I was to discover, sometimes familiar is not the best, or only, route.

I knew, that at age twenty-two, I would be one of the oldest women competing in gymnastics. Not that twenty-two is old by any means, but mine was a young person's sport. It had been difficult for me to get back into full training mode, especially after experiencing the freedom of "normal" life. It was a big adjustment from that kind of freedom to seven-hour training days, and a diet made up mostly of vegetables and lean proteins. I also went through months and months of extra conditioning and cardio. But I wanted another shot. I really did.

Why, you might ask? It's a simple question, and I asked it of myself several times. The answer, though, was not simple. Passion for the sport was part of it, as was ending my career on my terms, and I didn't think I was done yet. But the biggest part was that I wanted to drive myself one more time. I wanted to push myself as far as I could. I still wanted to see what I was made of. Someone else might have made a different decision. I knew there was no right or wrong here, but once I committed, I was in it all the way.

The 2012 Olympic Trials were going to be held the end of June at the HP Pavilion in San Jose, California and I was excited about the possibilities. Well, I was excited until very early in 2012 when I tore my rotator cuff and my labrum. The rotator cuff is actually a group of muscles and tendons all located next to each other that work to stabilize the shoulder, and the labrum is a piece of fibro cartilage that helps keep the ball of the shoulder joint in place. My tear was not caused by one single event, but was a combination of too much work on the bars over a long period of time. All that hanging and dangling over many years had taken its toll. This is a common injury for athletes, but it can be a devastating one. Unfortunately for me, these are very painful injuries.

My doctor determined that I needed surgery, but the operation is accompanied by a lengthy rehab. There was no way I'd be able to have the surgery and also prepare for the Olympic Trials. Time for another decision. After my doctor said that I probably would not injure the shoulder further if I continued to train, I chose to continue in that direction. I was warned that there would be pain, and there was, but I needed to try again, for me.

I had been so fortunate throughout my career to be treated by several amazing physicians who understood the special needs of an athlete. Dr. Daniel Cooper was one of these doctors, and was also the head team physician for the Dallas Cowboys. At the time of my injury, he was also the team physician for the Dallas Stars hockey team. He is an orthopedic surgeon who specializes in ankle and shoulder injuries. Dr. Larry Nassar was our USA Gymnastics National Team physician. He also spent twenty years as a certified athletic trainer, so had a good idea of the many demands on a gymnast's body.

Another person who assisted me tremendously was Dr. Vince Scheffler, a chiropractor who also helped me with physical therapy and massage therapy. In fact, without him, I'm not sure I would ever have gotten to the trials. I saw him three times a week for

months. He could not put my shoulder back together, only a surgeon could do that, but he definitely helped with the pain, and
with building whatever strength in the shoulder that I could.

Between these three doctors, and the additional help of
months of diet, exercise, and training, I got to the Olympic Trials.

Before I could get to the trials, though, I first had to compete
in several qualifying competitions and earn a score high enough
to make the grade. Along the way a number of people that I knew
tried to discourage me. "You can't do this," they said over, and
over. Whether their negativity had to do with my shoulder injury
or my "advanced" age, or their pessimism or plain old jealousy,
these people did not hesitate to let me know their feelings.

Wow. This was a different and surprising environment for
me. I had always been supported and lifted up by people I knew.
Then the media started to tear me down, too, in addition to some
of people around me. I'm happy that these people were not in
my inner circle, but even though I knew enough to stay true to
my goals, I struggled with their disapproval. On some days it was
very hard not to give in and believe the pessimistic words. Then
I'd have a good day at the gym, or I'd get a message from a fan and
my confidence in myself would be restored. This up and down
roller coaster of feelings and emotions continued for months, but
by the time the Olympic Trials came, I had learned to let most of
the negative words and the emotion they caused roll off my back.

I wished, though, that the words had never been said and still
feel that no one should ever try to tear down another person's
dreams. Who knows whether someone will ever achieve a big goal
or not, but it will be a lot harder to find success if no one else
believes in them. Even if the dream never becomes a reality, the
path to the goal will be filled with many valuable lessons and
experiences, and that is always worthwhile.

There were a lot of differences in preparing for these Olympic
Trials versus the one in 2008. In 2008 I was on a quest to achieve

my dream. Now I was the defending all-around champion. That meant there were a lot of eyes on me. Also, in 2008 I'd had the support of my family, friends, and a few fans. Now, there were people all across the world who were cheering me on—and these people outnumbered by far those who were trying to pull me off the podium. Before, I had not wanted to disappoint my parents, but in 2012, there were thousands of people I didn't even know whom I did not want to disappoint. I really wanted to show them one more time that hard work and perseverance pays off, and that whatever their own dreams were, they could achieve them.

Everything in 2012 hinged on two nights of competition. My bar routine was very difficult, but it was one that I had done thousands of times. I started out well and felt very, very confident. But about twenty-five seconds into the routine, I let go of the bar, flipped, twisted around, and when I came back toward the bar to grab it, I missed it and hit the ground hard, flat on my face.

In that instant, I knew my gymnastics career was over. Then a lot of things happened very quickly. After my body had absorbed the impact of the fall onto the hard mats, I pulled myself onto my knees. My dad, who had been spotting me rushed over. His first words spoke of his concern for me. "I'm okay," I told him, rolling my neck around. I wasn't really. My neck hurt and I later was found to have suffered a mild concussion, but I didn't know that then.

One of the first things a gymnast learns is how to fall. While the fall looked and sounded worse than it was, we are taught to fall flat, to avoid landing on a limb and breaking it. In the very last moment I knew I was not going to catch the bar or my dreams for that matter.

I was only thinking about the fall, but I can imagine the conflicted thoughts that were running through my dad's mind. As my coach and spotter, it was his job to catch me if I fell. But, if he touched me, even laid one finger on me when I could have actually caught the bar on my own, it was an automatic one-point deduction to my score. When scores are calculated in thousandths, a full point is a huge price to pay.

To catch me—or not? My dad only had a split second to make his decision, and up until the last instant even I thought I was going to catch the bar. I've watched the video of that fall many times, and if I had been in his shoes, I have to say that I would have made the same decision as he did. I am positive that even if he had caught me, I still would have fallen. Then we both would have gone down, and one or both of us could have gotten hurt.

I knew I had just thirty short seconds to get back up on the bars and finish my routine—if I chose to. Life is all about choices. I could have walked away, even walked out of the gym and all the way back to Texas, and no one would have faulted me for that choice. Well, no one but me. I knew that this was a decision I would have to live with for the rest of my life, and if I wanted to end my career on my terms I had to finish my routine. I also knew that if I completed this routine I would also have the courage to finish anything I ever started in my life. Besides, my dad had always taught me to finish what I started.

The crowd was eerily silent as I walked to re-chalk my hands. Then, when I walked back toward the bars they erupted into a deafening round of cheers. I had never heard anything like it before. The cheers were so loud that their echoes banged around inside my head and it was hard for me to think. I nodded at my dad and he boosted me back up onto the bars. And because I knew my career was over, I forgot about the competition. I forgot about the crowd, and my team. I forgot about the television cameras, photographers, and reporters. I finished that routine for my dad. He had been with me every step of the way, through all of the ups and down inside the gym and out. Whenever I faltered he'd always say, "Get up and go," so I did. I finished that routine and I have to say, I enjoyed every second of it.

At the end, I landed on my feet. Then I saluted to the judges, and the now silent crowd burst once again into rousing cheers. I was in total shock at their reaction. And when I looked up into the crowded arena, I saw almost twenty-thousand people on their feet. I was getting a standing ovation! Even all of the other coaches were clapping for me. So many emotions were flowing through me that I didn't know what to do. Tears formed and began to roll down my cheeks. I had just finished the absolute worst routine of my career, and these people still were supporting me. I waved to each section of the crowd and mouthed thank you. Their reaction was actually hard for me to comprehend. I loved what this wonderful group of spectators had done for me, but did not yet quite understand it. Then I saw my dad, went over to him, and hugged him for all the years of love and guidance that he had devoted to me.

I had never earned a standing ovation before. Not even when I won the all-around at the Olympics. I still find it very ironic that the first time people thought enough of my performance to stand up and clap for me was when I fell, splat, onto some very hard gymnasium mats.

My fall taught me more about life than an entire year in school ever could have. Most important was that when you literally or figuratively fall on your face, there are people out there who still love and support you. I had spent much of my career being worried that if I didn't win, that I would disappoint people. Now I knew that winning wasn't why they supported me. People supported my effort, my will to try, and my character. They supported *me.* That was an important distinction, and one I would carry forward with me, always.

As I walked to the sidelines I was at such peace. And, another, similar fear I had carried with me since 2008 disappeared. I had always wondered if people would still like me if I didn't do gymnastics. Did people like me for me, or did they like me for what I had accomplished? I realized then, that part of my wanting to take another shot at the Olympics was for that very reason. I hadn't wanted to let go of my gymnastics career, *because I had been afraid to.* I still had no idea who I was without the sport, or if people would still like me without it.

Then there was my wish to push myself as hard and as far as I could. My initial goal for that was another Olympic medal, but I had still reached that goal, just in a different way. To get back up on the bars, I had to push myself harder and farther than I ever had before. And my wish that people could see that hard work and dedication paid off? First, despite a debilitating and painful shoulder injury I was here at the US Olympic Trials. Not many gymnasts even get close to reaching this level of competition. Then, the audience had given me such a show of support. That alone did it for me. It was the perfect reward for my hard work.

These were all important thoughts, and I would have to think about them in depth, but right now there was no time. The next thing I knew I was in the arms of Liz Ballard, who had been standing backstage behind a curtain. Over the past six or so years, Liz had become a true best friend. I had met her through NBC, the network that aired the Olympics and some of the other national and international gymnastics competitions. Liz was the director of Olympic partnerships for NBC, but more important, she was the kind of person you meet who you click instantly with and know you will be friends forever.

As she hugged me, she said, "You don't realize it now, but this moment will define your life."

Liz was right, of course, but at that moment I was so embarrassed I wanted to crawl under a rock. There were so many things swirling around in my brain, so many thoughts and emotions that I couldn't grasp onto any of them. I will say that getting back up on the bars and finishing my routine took more courage than anything I've ever done in my life. And, I am more proud of that one, single action than anything else I have ever accomplished.

The reason I fell was that I had missed completing a skill called a Gienger release. The move looks like a back layout fly away followed by a half turn above the bar, then the gymnast comes back down to catch the same bar. It was a move that I had been doing since I was eleven, and I found a lot of irony in it. In my very first national championship competition, the one in Cleveland, Ohio just after I made the junior national team when I was twelve, I had fallen off the bars doing a Gienger release.

Whoever would have guessed that the cause of the fall that started my national competitions would also end it? Yes, the Gienger release both started and ended my ten-year competitive career. You could not get more full circle than that.

Except, my career wasn't quite over. Not just yet. I still had to perform a routine on the balance beam. My dad mentioned to me that I didn't have to do this, but I wanted to. Even though half the people in the arena expected me to fall again, I knew that I couldn't—and wouldn't. It was important for me to end my career on a high note. Not that a standing ovation isn't huge praise, but I wanted my last competitive routine to be as flawless as possible.

This last routine I did for me. I should have been filled with conflicted emotion, but all I felt during the routine was the pure, simple joy of the performance. During my lifetime, I had spent many thousands of hours on the beam, and now I only wanted the pleasure of performing on it one last time. Those few minutes were, in my mind, perfection. And no, I did not fall. Instead, I was once more the little girl I had been when I was three, filled with the wonderment of performing a skill on the beam.

That mindset took away all of the pressure that is usually associated with competition. For me, there was no medal, no team to worry about. There was just me—and my love for the sport. The performance did not count in the greater scheme of gymnastics, but it was of huge importance to me. Actually, I think of it as one of the best routines I ever did. After, I once again waved to the crowd, and the people once more left their seats to give me a second standing ovation. It was as if they knew I was saying good-bye.

My farewell wave was another precious moment that I will never forget. The appreciation that the fans showed to me made everything worthwhile, and validated me in a way that I never expected. Looking back, it took a lot of guts and courage, but I am so proud that I finished both of my routines. Sometimes, out of the ashes of disaster come the best moments in life.

❦

After the 2012 trials I knew I no longer had to worry that the physical demands of my sport might put my body in jeopardy. That knowledge was a relief, but it was also bittersweet. When one door closes, however, another opens. My thought of somehow, someway being in London for the 2012 Games soon became a reality. I attended as the female athlete representative for the International Gymnastics Federation.

Being the athlete rep was an enormous honor, as gymnasts from across the world elected me to be the go-between for the gymnasts and the Olympic committee. If any of the gymnasts had a problem with the competition, my job was to talk to the women's technical committee and help get it worked out. I was also asked to join the NBC Olympic broadcasting team in London, and did a few other interviews and special events throughout the Games. It was a big role, and I took it on with the greatest of pride.

It was, I admit, a bit difficult not to be competing at the event, as that had been my initial goal. The saving grace for me was that I knew without doubt that I had given my all at the trials and also in the weeks and months leading up to it. All you can do is your very best, and that is exactly what I had done. Competing here in London, for me, was just not to be. My parents had also stayed home this trip, so I was on my own at the Olympics for the first time. Even in the moment I knew that this trip was the beginning of an exciting, new part of life for me, and it was something that I welcomed with open arms.

Chapter Ten

In an odd way, after the 2012 Olympic Trials I did not feel as lost as I had after the 2008 Olympics. I still wasn't sure what was going to come next, but I wasn't as nervous about my future as I had been before. If I looked for opportunities, I knew they would come, and they did.

In thinking about my future, I knew education would be part of it. I had always wanted to finish college and while the specifics of that dream had been vague, now I knew I wanted to get a degree in sports management.

I still could not see a life for myself completely outside of gymnastics or the Olympics, and once I ended the competitive side of the sport for myself, I realized there were other places where I could fit in. Coaching was one option, and I was sure that a spot could be made for me at WOGA. I also could become a sports agent, a person who manages the careers of athletes. There were product development careers in the field of gymnastics equipment or fashion, and then there was sports broadcasting and commentating. Those were just a few of the many possibilities, but I knew that a degree in sports management would set me up for whatever direction I ended up going.

Liz Ballard had become an excellent sounding board over the years. Even though I was in Dallas and she was based in New York, we texted and Facebooked back and forth all the time. Whenever I was in New York we enjoyed our quality girl time together. Over the years, I had been in New York more often than you might think, either for competitions, events, or sponsor meetings.

One reason the friendship between Liz and me grew is that she understood my world. She had worked for NBC for ten years, and during that time was involved in the coverage of seven different Olympic Games. She knew I had to focus 100 percent on my career when I was competing, because she was part of the arm of the network that often covered my sport. She got *it*, and she got me. That meant she did not put demands on our growing friendship that I could not meet, and understood when I disappeared for days and weeks at a time into my daily routine of training. Some of my other friendships had dropped by the wayside because they didn't understand all of my many commitments, but over time, Liz became the older sister I never had.

Oddly enough, Liz was from New Orleans, so we had that in common, too. Because Liz was based in New York City and had attended New York University (NYU), I began to look at their sports management degree program, the same degree program Liz had gone through. Even though I would be an "older" student who had some life experience, I found the thought of starting school in a new city quite daunting. Having a friend like Liz close by could help ease my transition.

After I spoke to school officials at NYU, though, I was sure that this was where I needed to be. Many of their courses were hands on and practical in nature, versus theoretical, and I liked that. It was one thing to hear and read about developing a plan for a sports team, for example, but it was quite another to write your own business plan, which was part of the course work.

So, I applied and crossed my fingers. Not everyone gets in at their first choice of schools, so I was thrilled when I was accepted—especially as I had not applied anywhere else. Once the decision about NYU was final, though, I began to see the big picture reality of it all. When I had moved out of my parents' home in Texas I was nineteen, and was living close by. I could drive to the gym or hang out at my parent's dining table anytime I wanted. But a move more than a thousand miles away was downright frightening.

For almost twenty years my parents and I had been a team, Team Liukin. We'd had the same dream, the same goal, the same everything. My dad was the coach, I was the athlete, and my mom was the rock and the glue that held us all together. As you can imagine, the end of my athletic career and my moving away was a big adjustment for all of us. Both my mom and dad said they missed seeing me in the gym every day, and I missed being there, too. My mom has also said that she took great joy in watching me train and perform, and that she felt sadness that she would no longer be able to do that.

Yes, a chapter in my life had closed, but we all had known from the beginning that this time would eventually come. Gymnasts do not continue competing forever. My parents, however, had raised me to be a strong, independent young woman. I couldn't say that I was there yet, but I knew if I was to reach that particular goal, then New York City was the perfect place for me to start the next chapter of my life.

For starters, I had always been intrigued about the city. It was so vital and alive, and there was always so much going on. New Yorkers themselves seemed to be very focused, caring, independent and spirited people, and the energy of the city was so electric that I eventually realized I had found a second home. I also loved that New York was a city filled with people who were physically fit from walking everywhere. There isn't much room for a car in Manhattan, so people walk. I was giddy with excitement, and in January of 2013 I began my new adventure.

I quickly found an apartment near Union Square, not too far from NYU. One of my requirements in finding an apartment was location. I knew I might not get everything I wanted: updated kitchen, large closets, extra bedroom, good storage space. This was New York after all and space was always at a premium. However, location was of prime importance because I would not have a car in the city. I also was not comfortable riding the subway regularly. Somewhere along the path of life I realized that I was a little bit claustrophobic, and tight, dark places made me feel very uncomfortable. So, I needed to be able to walk to school, and to places where I could get groceries.

Even though I was eager to start my new adventure, as soon as I moved in I wondered what in the world I had gotten myself into. When the reality of it all sunk in, I realized again how terrified I was. Plus, it really was much harder than I had expected for me to not see my parents every day. Because my family had been a closely-knit unit that worked together, ate together, and played together all day, every day, that transition was harder on me than it might have been for someone else. I also missed my little Ella and our other dogs terribly, as well as the laid back atmosphere of Texas. Dallas truly is home for me and I felt very lost and alone.

Besides being homesick, New York had a huge snowstorm the first week I was there. I, of course, had seen snow before, had even spent a few minutes here and there playing in it. But living with mounds of the stuff 24/7? No. Between the homesickness, snow, and the very cold temperatures, I called my dad and told him I wanted to come home. In his infinite wisdom, he said no.

"You've signed a lease on an apartment for one year," he reminded me. "You need to stay and finish what you started. When you come home for Christmas in December, and if you still feel the same way, then we can decide what to do."

I knew he was right and I listened to his wise words as I always did, but I can't say I was all that happy about it. Now I can see how these challenging experiences made me more mature and responsible. All of the great morals and ethics that my parents had instilled into me from day one, all of the memorable things my mom and dad had said to me over the years, they were finally becoming useful to me. I also have wondered how hard that must have been for my dad, to know that I wanted with all of my being to come home, and for him to say no. I can see that sometimes the job of a parent can be very hard.

Of course I couldn't run out on my lease, or quit school. I hadn't given either a chance. And, I if let a little (okay, a lot) of snow run me out of town, I wasn't a very strong person. I hung in there, and I sure am glad that I did! My new life wasn't always easy, and my feeling of being lost and directionless continued for some time, but each day brought me closer to an exciting future in sports that I could almost reach out and touch.

One of the biggest adjustments for me was learning to live without a car. In Texas, if I needed groceries I drove to a big store, got them, came home, and carried in three or four shopping bags. In New York City, however, I could only buy what I could carry, and I often had to go to several places to get what I needed. That first year I was there, fruit came from the street vendor on the corner, food from the little store on the corner, and toiletries from the pharmacy on the next block. On my first shopping trip I bought far too much and struggled to lug it all home. It was a very different way of living, but one that I eventually got used to.

The idea of starting classes was also exciting to me, but some of my old insecurities about fitting in came rushing back on my first day. Many of my fellow students were eighteen or nineteen years old. Here I was at the ripe old age of twenty-four. Five or six years of life experience in older people does not mean much, but I found that the difference in maturity, experience, and perspective between the ages of eighteen and twenty-four can be enormous. I really felt like I didn't fit in; I felt so out of place.

To compound the differences, I also was far more traveled than most of my fellow students and had seen far more of the world. I had been involved in many business negotiations with my sponsors and had given a ton of interviews. While my focus was on learning, networking, and grades, my other classmates also had strong interests in concerts, parties, and just plain hanging out. I am not knocking any of those activities, but I had little interest in them and even less time. In addition to school, I had broadcasting duties with NBC, and sponsor and Olympic obligations. I often wondered if I could be any more different than the kids who sat in the same classrooms as I did.

With all that said, making friends was harder than I had expected it to be. Going in, I had decided to keep a low profile. Yes, I was an Olympic gold medalist. Yes, many of my students and professors had seen me on television, and either rooted for or against me during my gymnastics career. But I wanted to put all of that in the background and just be Nastia. It turned out that was not possible. Well, at least not all of the time.

I've mentioned before how important it is to have positive friends who support you. It turned out that at NYU many of the students knew of my background and I made a few stumbling steps when I realized that one or two of my new friends liked me for what I had done in the sport, rather than liked me for me. This had been one of my fears: that some people would just want to hang onto the coattails of a very minor celebrity. The realization that my fear had become a reality made me withdraw. It took some time and a few motivational talks with myself before I reached out again.

My new strategy when it came to possible friends was, rather than to try to incorporate everyone I met into my busy life, I hoped to meet one new friend in every class, or during every semester. It turned out that strategy has worked well for me and over the past few years I have developed some strong friendships. One of those friends is Jenny Kwon. She has been a great friend to me since we met during my sophomore year at NYU. Even though she has since graduated, we still keep in touch and see each other whenever we can.

Another issue in making friends was that many of the students lived on campus. NYU has twenty-three residence halls that house eleven thousand students. That's as big as some small towns. As with our gymnastic team training camps, there is camaraderie in college life that develops when you share experiences, such as dorm food, walking to class, the rules of a particular residence, and even in everyday proximity to each other.

I had chosen to live off campus for many reasons, but mostly because I still had a lot of professional responsibilities to juggle, along with my new life as a college student. I sometimes needed to leave very early in the morning or come home very late at night and I thought that might be disruptive to my dorm roommates. Another reason was my studies. I was used to studying in a quiet, solitary environment, rather than the more hectic environment of a dorm. And, when it came to cramming for a test, I was never one to pull an all-nighter.

My regular sleep schedule had not varied much since my athletic training days. I still got up early and went to bed early. I knew that most college students stayed up later than I did and got much less sleep than I was used to. I did not want my differences to impose on either set of schedules—theirs or mine. So between my career, sleep and study habits, living off campus, and busy schedule, it was difficult for me to get to know people.

A final consideration when it came to friendships had to do with community. When I was growing up, most of my friends came from the gym. My parents knew their parents, and sometimes their grandparents. My school friends and I all lived near each other, and most of us were in the same economic and social categories. We also often agreed about social issues or current events of the day.

As I moved into my teens and expanded my competitive career, my parents still knew many of the coaches and parents of the people that I hung out with. In that way my life was almost like it was for people years ago, with young adults marrying others from the same community, and the parents, grandparents (and sometimes even the great-grandparents) all knew each other.

There is something safe and wonderful in that kind of situation, but NYU was completely the opposite. There I found people from many different backgrounds, cultures, religions, and socio/economic statuses wanting to befriend me. All that was great, as I had a lot of experience with languages, and with people from other parts of the world. What tripped me up, though, was that this was the first time I had gotten to be around a lot of different people without also knowing members of their family, their other friends, where they grew up, and all those other things that give two people a level of familiarity on their first meeting.

Then, when I did find someone I thought I'd like to get to know better, I had no idea what to talk about. Small talk has never been one of my strengths. That's why I totally get it when kids I meet at my speaking events tell me they don't feel like they fit in. I've been there, over and over again. Thinking back to my early days at NYU, I would have been far more comfortable in a business meeting with a potential sponsor than in a classroom of twenty fellow students.

I definitely made some mistakes with my friendships. A mistake is not the worst thing in the world, but a mistake with a prospective new friend can also bring emotional hurt. I didn't have the time or energy for that and the result was that I was slow to make friends at my new school.

The biggest thing that helped ease my anxiety about friendships and my directionless feelings was my classes. Most people get nervous about their academic performance, but I have always loved learning. College is as much about learning about life as it is the classroom work, and while I struggled with the former at first, I embraced the latter.

Because I had been out in the real world, I could see how useful the ideas I was learning in my accounting, business development, and other classes were. Many of our professors on the sports management side held full time jobs in the sports industry, so those classes were often held at night. What an amazing thing it was to learn from people who were actually in the business. Not that academic theory is not important, too, but to hear real life, behind the scenes stories about the business side of sports from people who had experienced them first hand was incredible. I learned so much from that kind of a setting, important lessons about human nature that I will definitely carry with me into the future.

When I tell people I am pursuing a career in sports management, some ask me why I even bothered to go to school. They even remind me that I had a lot of personal experience in elite-level sports. But the Olympic world is different from collegiate sports, which is different from professional team sports. All have different cultures, rules, and seasons, and each is structured a little differently on the business end. I wanted to learn all I could about all sports, not just Olympic events.

The networking opportunities that I found within my major were also very important. Not to get too clichéd, but there is another saying: it's not what you know, but who you know. In many cases that is true. Through my studies at NYU, I have met many of the movers and shakers in the sports world: agents, managers, and people who work in executive management positions with sports teams. Those kinds of connections are invaluable. Just as you might go to my dad (who is one of the top gymnastic coaches in the world) if you want to excel in that sport, I wanted to meet the top business people in my chosen field. That concept of meeting and learning from the top people works no matter what it is you want to do. If you look hard enough, there are always ways to find and to meet the most successful people in your field, and then learn from them.

In one other way my classes helped me fit in and make friends. From time to time one of my professors asked me about my specific experience as it related to something we were talking about in class. It might be working with a sponsor, or the realities of team travel. My experiences then often started a lively class discussion. Not only did I meet a few new friends that way, friends who liked me for me, but I also felt validated. I had finally found a place where I could talk about my competitive days, where people would acknowledge it, discuss it, find a lesson or two in my mishaps and successes, and move on.

As the years go by I have found that I am much more than just my Olympic experiences or sport. Everyone is. We all have depths, multiple interests, opinions, and experiences that go way beyond whatever it is we might be best known for. You are much more than a boss, daughter, or a science whiz. You are more than the volleyball star, or the violin prodigy. It was so refreshing for me to be able to finally find friends that I could bake cookies or watch movies with and not once ever talk about the Olympics. Not that I didn't want to discuss them, I just didn't want to talk about them all day every day. You are probably the same in wanting to talk about many different topics with many different people.

While I was very lost and lonely my first year or so at NYU, I am so glad that my dad encouraged me to stay. Today I feel very comfortable in New York and at school. My collegiate days have opened so many new doors, and I have made many great friends and learned a lot about life. I have also come to love the hustle and bustle of New York City. It just took me a little longer than it might have another person.

And when that first year rolled around and my apartment lease was up? No, I didn't renew the lease, but I did move to a different apartment. I felt that my time in New York might be limited to the years I was in school there, so I decided to experience a different area of the city each year. While it was a bit of a hassle to move every twelve months, it was a great way to discover the many different flavors of the city.

My first year in New York taught me not to give up on things too soon. Had I given up on New York and my education there, I would have missed out one of the greatest experiences of my life. I don't regret one thing about my education or my many experiences in New York—except the very cold weather!

Chapter Eleven

Outside of school I maintained a busy schedule in New York, even that first year, but I always found time to work out. Exercise is important to the wellness of the body, so I wanted to make sure I was doing all the right things to keep me strong and healthy. Besides, a daily workout had been ingrained into me for so many years that I felt odd if I skipped a day.

The problem was, I had led such a structured training schedule for so many years, that I didn't know how to work out without someone telling me what to do. You'd think that over the years I would have absorbed some sense of "what comes next" when it came to exercise, but no. Part of it was that I was no longer a competitive gymnast, so all of the exercises I had done to prepare me for the balance beam, bars, and floor exercise events were no longer relevant.

Plus, many of the gyms I visited in New York did not have the gymnastic equipment I was used to. Instead of uneven bars and a big, open area of floor mats, there were weight machines, treadmills, and exercise bikes. So, along with the rest of my life, I was absolutely lost when it came to fitness, too. Ironic, right? An Olympian who doesn't know how to exercise. To counter-act my feelings I started to explore fitness opportunities and workouts that were outside my level of expertise.

Fortunately, in New York, there were many options close to my apartment, and at various times that worked into my odd schedule. In my explorations I took yoga, spinning, and then Pilates. Then I tried a boot camp-style fitness class. Whatever I could find that I had not tried before, I did—and I found that I loved something about every new sport or activity that I tried. Going in, I knew that my entire time in New York would be about learning, and this included my life outside of school. From the many cultures New York has to offer, to living in a big city, to things I was discovering about myself, this was an important time in my life.

Another goal of mine was to meet people outside of gymnastics. For most of my life, almost everyone I knew was involved in the sport. From coaches to friends, to parents of friends, everyone was all about gymnastics. That was great immersion while I was focused on my goal of winning a medal at the Olympics. But for me to learn and grow as a person, it was important that I meet a lot of different kinds of people.

School, of course, provided much of that, but I also met a variety of people in the many fitness classes that I took. And there were certainly a lot of people to get to know. There are more than eight million people living in the city. If I wanted to meet people, this was certainly the place to be.

Meeting so many new people, each with passions and goals of their own, helped me put my many loose ends into perspective. As you might imagine, with the background I had it was very hard for me to not know what my next ten years looked like. There were many days where I came home from school in tears, which might simply have been emotion spilling out from all of my new experiences, rather than frustration with life, although there was some of that, too.

One of my frustrations was that as much as I wanted it to be, mine was not the life of the typical college student. I still had commitments to many of my sponsors, and to USA Gymnastics and the US Olympic Committee. Those commitments meant a lot of emails, meetings, and public appearances, but I was so pleased that I could still in some way be part of gymnastics and the Olympics. I never wanted that part of my life to end. I still don't.

Many great opportunities came my way during those years after the Olympics. Some of them I grabbed onto and others, for a variety of reasons, I let pass me by. My involvement in each project was decided on a case-by-case basis, and in addition to my own feelings about an opportunity, I also considered the input of my manager and my parents. The project not only had to fit me, it also had to fit my personality and interests, and the timing had to be right. Too much going on at any one time meant nothing would get done. Didn't want that to happen!

A manager first represented me when I was about fifteen. I had been getting a lot of interest from potential sponsors, and had a lot of requests from exhibitions for personal appearances. While I would have liked to show up at every event that wanted me to come to say a few words or to sign autographs, it wasn't feasible. First, my parents and I could not afford to fly around the country doing this with no compensation, and second, the timing had to be right so as not to interfere too much with my training, or with school.

My mom and dad had always felt uncomfortable talking about money when it came to my gymnastics career, especially when many of the offers came from people they knew and thought of as friends. Whether it was a sponsor or the owner of a gym, it was likely that my mom and dad knew the person well. My parents wanted to do what was right for me and that became hard when they were also dealing with friends. It was awkward for my dad, for example, to ask for more money for me, and then he felt guilty if he didn't.

It was also difficult for my mom or dad to limit the terms of my appearances when they were dealing with people they knew as friends. One person might want me to sign autographs and hang around the gym for six hours, for example, when two or three hours would be plenty of time for me to see and talk to everyone who came out.

So, when the number of offers and the logistics of the few they accepted began to take time away from my training and their duties at WOGA, they were just as glad to turn that part of my career over to a manager.

We met with several managers who had approached us in the past, and we listened to their ideas about how they would handle the business side of my career. My parents and I would still have final say on every decision, but having someone else field the offers and negotiate the details would be a big help. Eventually, we chose a manager. Over the course of my career, as it grew and expanded I needed different things, so I moved on several times and had new managers to cover the different stages.

A few of the projects that were being offered to me post-Olympics came about as a result of things I had done before. Acting roles were one of these. In 2006, my dad and I had the chance to become involved with the poplar gymnastics movie, *Stick It*. The movie was a teen comedy that followed a group of underdogs and "mean girls" on their journey to an invitational meet. On the way they find injustice, and unite to fight it.

Mine was just a brief appearance where I did a bar routine during a competition and my dad was my coach. The producers had wanted me to have a larger role (and I wanted that, too!). But, that would have taken too much time away from my training before the 2008 Olympics and I chose to keep training hard. The tiny role was fun, though, and I loved learning about acting and how movies were made. It was the first occasion I'd had to spend time in front of the camera doing something other than an interview, and I liked it.

The biggest problem was that it is the nature of filming to shoot a scene over and over again to get it just right. That meant that I had to do endless takes of my bar routine, and each take left me more tired than the last. Even then, I was doing a very demanding routine and it was difficult both on a mental and a physical level to execute it perfectly. Finally my dad stepped in and said we had to stop, that I was getting too tired. The funny thing was that the producers and crew were surprised that doing my routine was so exhausting. "You make it look so easy," one of them said. That was the ultimate compliment, but it didn't help my aching arms and muscles.

My part in the movie only took a few days away from my training schedule, and I was okay with that. I knew that if I wanted to pursue acting, there would be other opportunities after the Olympics. And, there were.

Just after the 2008 Games I was eating dinner with a few of my friends in Los Angeles. As only happens in LA, the producers of the CW drama *Gossip Girl* (2007-2012) were sitting next to us. The show followed the lives of privileged teenagers on New York's upper east side, along with the blogger who was always watching them. When I was in high school, it happened to be one of my favorite shows.

Before we finished our meal, the producers sent over a note on a napkin via the waiter. It read: CONGRATS ON THE GOLD . . . KEEP WATCHING GOSSIP GIRL. XOXO. I was thrilled with the note, but even happier to hear that they called my manager the next day to ask if I wanted to do a guest appearance on the show. Did I? Of course I did! I ended up with a cameo in Season 2, Episode 12. I only had a few seconds and one line in a party scene, but it was a ton of fun.

While my experiences with acting have been minimal so far, I have come to appreciate the time and attention actors put into their craft, as well as the dedication of the behind-the-scenes people. Much like sports, acting is another example of how working hard to keep your end goal in sight often pays off very well.

Life is so interesting, as one experience seems to prepare us all for the next. My spot in *Stick It* absolutely prepared me for *Gossip Girl*. And, when it comes to the tougher aspects of our individual journeys, the same holds true. We may not know why we have to go through a difficult or stressful time when it is happening, but after, we can often see the purpose behind it all. Beyond the Olympics, one of my wishes was to be able to give back to the sport. I can now see that each of my injuries, and my disappointments in some of my competitions, happened for a reason. I needed to have experienced those things so I could better understand the highs and lows that come on the road to achievement of any big goal.

⚬⚬⚬

I remember when I was growing up, my favorite gymnast was Lilia Podkopayeva. She won the all-around title at the 1995 World Championships, and then went on to become the all-around champion at the 1996 Olympic Games. Like me, she was known for her poetic style and her graceful movements.

Lilia was, in every sense of the word, my hero, and I wanted to be just like her. When I learned that my dad knew her, and her coach, and had also arranged for me to meet her, I was beside myself. When we actually met, I didn't know what to say. I was that overcome. But she was friendly and kind, and made a huge and positive impression on me. Every hero should be as perfect in a little girl's eyes.

Years later, I was reminded of Lilia when I saw my name on the big sign outside of Cowboy Stadium (now known at AT&T Stadium) in Arlington, Texas. A wonderful giving-back prospect had come my way, and this one was very near and dear to my heart. I was thrilled to partner with USA Gymnastics to create the Nastia Liukin Cup. I hoped that my time talking with the young gymnasts at this event would inspire them to reach for their dreams, no matter what they were, just as Lilia inspired me to reach for mine when I was a young girl. I was excited, because this was my chance to provide an inspiring and competitive opportunity for hopeful Olympic gymnasts in the United States.

Any proceeds from the cup would go into the Nastia Liukin Fund, a charitable fund that was created within the National Gymnastics Foundation. In the very first year of the event we were able to give back, and the Nastia Liukin Fund gave scholarships to young gymnasts who showed great ability, but who had financial hardship. I have to say that there is no better feeling than lending a helping hand to a deserving person.

The Nastia Liukin Cup is held the Friday night before the American Cup and gymnasts are only invited to attend after they participate in and place in the top two in one of the twenty to thirty preliminary competitions across the country. For some girls, this will be the biggest event they ever compete in. For others it will just be a stepping-stone toward much greater successes. Gabby Douglas, who won gold medals in both the individual all-around and team competition at the 2012 Olympics, has competed in the Nastia Liukin Cup, as have three of the girls from the 2015 World Championship team. The best part about the event is that it is a great chance for me to meet so many talented girls and to give them a few words of encouragement. Prior to the competition, I am also able to spend time with each of the girls during a special brunch and dinner for all of the competitors.

On top of the Nastia Liukin Cup, one of my dreams had been to move into broadcasting, and the many professional connections I had made at NBC during my competitive years eventually led to a broadcasting role. In 2012, along with my duties as the athletes' representative for the Olympic Games in London, I served as a contributor to NBCOlympics.com coverage. Later, I also reported for NBC Olympics' coverage of the Olympic Winter Games, which were held in February of 2014 in Sochi, Russia. Every day of the competition I presented features for *The Olympic Zone*, a thirty-minute daily show that aired on all of the NBC affiliate stations. It was a great opportunity, because I got to cover all aspects of the Games, not just gymnastics. It was also amazing for me to be back in Russia.

I now serve as the lead female analyst for all of NBC's gymnastics coverage, including the P&G Championships, world championships, AT&T American Cup and the Olympic Games. It is such an exciting job and I'm so honored to be the female voice of gymnastics for all of those watching at home.

That said, being in front of the camera is not as easy as it looks. I remember the first time I did commentary for NBC. I made a big mistake when I answered live, on-camera, a question that the producer asked me on my earpiece. After a moment of silence he said quietly into my ear, "Just so you know, everyone watching just heard what you said."

Talk about humiliation! I was mortified. Despite my initial instinct to clap my hands over my mouth in embarrassment, I composed myself and went on with the broadcast. The overall result must have turned out okay, though, as instead of firing me, they gave me a contract to do more.

As you might imagine, there is a lot more to live coverage than just standing in front of a camera. I do a lot of research and homework on individual gymnasts, both men and women. To speak intelligently to the millions of people watching on live television—and to keep the audience intrigued and entertained—I need to combine the depth of my knowledge of the sport with interesting facts about the competitors as people. I never really know where a conversation will take me, or what might happen in the middle of a routine, so I have to be well prepared, and that is something I take very seriously.

When I was competing I had never paid much attention to men's gymnastics. The fact was, I had enough trouble keeping up with my own side of the sport. But now I have to be equally as well versed in what the guys are doing as I am in keeping up with the women. Getting up to speed on all of this definitely was a huge learning curve, as the men have different rules and equipment, and even the names of their skills are different than the women's. There were a number of athletes whom I did not know very well, and I had to learn each gymnast's strengths and weaknesses as well as the details of their background. And I had to learn it all well enough to spout it off as easily if I was talking about the weather.

I love being in this area of the sport, though, especially because it involves educating people about something I love. Many people do not understand the intricacies of gymnastics, and the more of us who can educate others about what the gymnasts are doing, the more that spectators will begin to follow the gymnasts, and the sport in general. There is room for a lot of growth in gymnastics, and the bigger we get, the better we can support young, talented gymnasts.

The other Olympic project I am currently excited about is being the athlete spokesperson for the "Road to Rio." This is a series of fun events in various cities across the country designed to get people fired up about the 2016 Summer Games in Rio de Janeiro. The tour goes across the country from July 2015 to August 2016. Due to school and a few other commitments, I won't be able to make all of the stops, but I will be there for most of them. It will be another fun way for me to interact with fans and get to meet them one-on-one.

These are just a small sampling of the many projects and events I have been involved with during the past few years. And you know what? It all came about as a result of hard work and dedication. The other thing is that in our media driven society, in a society that is focused on immediate gratification, people often see the end result, but the long hours of practice and the ups and downs of reaching the goal are ignored.

Some of the people that I meet, both young and old, seem lost. They have no goal, and no concept of the long hours of focused attention it will take to make a dream become a reality. I struggled, too, after the Olympics. I had no goal and was so lost. I had no idea what came next, or what I should be doing. It was a hard and difficult time for me, and my heart breaks for people who struggle through those tough periods in their lives.

I don't know everything, but I have come far enough in life to know that you have to have a goal. You also have to have a plan for the goal and an end result in mind. You do not have to become an Olympic champion, and your goal does not have to take fifteen years to achieve. But if you want a promotion, to earn an A in math, or to buy your dream house, you have to commit to the goal, and then break that goal into baby steps. Of course you have to focus a good deal of attention on each step. But before long you will see progress, and people will become interested in you and in helping you achieve success.

My "lost" period lasted several years, off and on. But, these post-Olympic projects that came my way helped me find where I needed to be. And, an old friendship and a new conviction came together in a very unique way to give me a new goal, one that I was amazingly excited about.

Chapter Twelve

(O)ver time, the path I wanted to take for the next years of my life became clear. For me, it was all about giving back. Gymnastics had given me so much that I wanted to pass along every bit of the poise, confidence, balance, coordination, determination, responsibility, social skills, and the many other things that I had learned through the sport.

My classes, professors, and fellow students at NYU were an enormous help in assisting me in find my way. Maybe not directly, but through class discussions I started to think about their shared thoughts and ideas, and realized that I somehow wanted to work to inspire and empower other young girls..

One class discussion became especially interesting and I have thought about it often. It was on the topic of performance enhancing drugs in competition. I was surprised and shocked when one of my classmates strongly supported the use of these drugs, and again when our professor did not actively disagree. My classmate's reasoning was that everyone was using them, so to be competitive everyone else must use them, too. I absolutely disagree.

First, in any Olympic sport, even at lower levels, any athlete who is on a US team whether it is gymnastics, track and field, swimming, skating, skiing, or other such sport are drug tested at random throughout the year. When I was competing I had to let the USA Gymnastics know where I was twenty-four hours a day, seven days a week, and I knew that they could test me anywhere, at any time.

If I was going on vacation, I had to let them know when and where. Flying to a sponsor meeting? I had to let them know what hotel I was staying in and what my schedule was. Once, the people who did the drug testing showed up at my house at six in the morning. In another instance, I was tested three times in the same week when they came to WOGA looking for me. There is a long list of banned substances in my sport and I was always careful to comply with that list. Never, ever, did I test positive.

Even if I had ever thought about taking a performing enhancing drug, there was no way I could coordinate the drug use with the 24/7 unannounced drug testing visits—not to mention my strong belief that you should always earn something on your own merits. I never wanted to look back and wonder if it was the drug that won a medal, or if I had actually earned it through my own hard work and dedication. There is no pride or honesty in a person who cheats both themselves and the public when they take banned substances. Even the thought of taking something to achieve a goal disgusts me. Whatever happened to the concept of working harder to become better, faster, and stronger?

I have no personal experience with professional team sports such as baseball, basketball, football, or hockey. But from the number of player suspensions, banned substances are obviously being used. In Olympic-level sports the fine for testing positive the first time is a two-year suspension. That's two years of sitting on the sidelines while your competitors progress in their level of skill. Testing positive the second time results in a lifetime ban from the sport you worked years to succeed in; a lifetime ban from a sport you loved.

Unfortunately, in professional sports the penalties are much less. Depending on the sport, a first time positive test might mean a suspension of a few games. A second offense? The athlete sits out a few more games. The penalties are so low they are ridiculous. As you can see, I am violently opposed to any kind of drug, performance enhancing or otherwise, and can't imagine any situation where I would consider tarnishing my body by using them.

At our discussion at school, I became outraged when the professor mentioned to me that I might feel otherwise if I was a professional athlete and millions of dollars were at stake. That's when the awkwardness set in yet again. As I mentioned, at school I didn't always tell people who I was. Many of my classmates knew, because they had either followed gymnastics or seen me compete at the Olympics or broadcasting for NBC. And, some students had been in other classes of mine where my gymnastics career had come up for discussion. But not all of my classmates knew, and certainly not all of my professors—including this one. In my effort to fit in, I usually preferred that my background stay in the background, but now I felt compelled to speak out. So I did.

I told the class, and the professor, about the realities of Olympic-level sports. I told them of the random drug testing, the financial side of how athletes worked with sponsors, of income earned from product endorsements, and of the life-changing suspensions for minor drug violations. I'm not sure everyone was swayed toward my point of view, especially the student whose views started the discussion, but I'm glad the subject came up because it is an important one. Nothing beats hard work, focus, and dedication toward your goal. And if you cheat with drugs, you only cheat yourself.

❧

About that same time, life delivered another of its little quirks when Liz said she might like to join me in my newest venture, whatever it turned out to be. Seriously! I could not have been more excited. Liz had years of senior level project management under her belt, lots of business and industry contacts, and enough experience to launch any idea with flying colors. I was so glad that she was ready for a change in her professional life and wanted to work with me. Besides, I was once more ready for a new manager, and she would be fabulous in that role as well.

My business classes at school had taught me that I would need help in achieving my new goals, just as I had needed help in reaching my Olympic goals. I did not win my Olympic medals on my own. Without my coaches (including my mom and dad, Sergei, Yevgeny and several others who helped early on), and my doctors, therapists, friends, sponsors, and other supporters, I never would have made it to the Olympics. In developing a new business or idea, it is the same. It is almost impossible to do it all completely by yourself. Well, at least it is difficult to do everything perfectly, and from financing to web design to marketing I did not want to leave any stone unturned.

Plus, there are only so many hours in the day and I was still a college student. But, I knew I was biting off a big chunk of something exciting. If I was to become effective in my dream of impacting young girls, in inspiring them to become all they could be, Liz was the perfect person to help me on this journey. I had known her since I was about sixteen, so there would be no surprises in her personality or background that might derail us in our efforts to work with each other. Years of spending time together had taken care of that. How cool was it that best friends could work together to develop interesting projects and also have fun together?

The two of us brainstormed for months. We both wanted to impact girls of all ages in a way that was personal and interactive. For years, my fan interaction had been limited to sitting behind a table and signing autographs. Sometimes that was all that an event allowed. There might not be enough space at a venue to do more, or there could be time constraints on the use of the space or the table, or the athlete might also have other commitments he or she had to go to. I knew that, because I'd been there many times. However, the typical autograph format did not allow much time for one-on-one discussions, and I always left feeling unsatisfied.

Liz had also witnessed plenty of occasions when I had done the autograph thing as part of an event and said, "I see girls who just want to ask you one question, but there is no time." I thought about that, and agreed.

Late October of 2014 found the two of us in an airplane, flying from New York to Florida to spend a few days with my parents to celebrate my twenty-fifth birthday. During the flight we came to the conclusion that the best way to get individual time with the girls was for me to travel to them. I could see and meet them on their own turf, in a place that was comfortable for them: a gym.

We also thought it would be helpful to break each individual tour stop into two parts. The first part would be a more formal presentation, with me talking about my career interspersed with video clips from the Olympics—clips of my gold medal winning performance and of me falling on my face. It was important to me for these girls to know that my entire career had not always been full of sunshine and glamour. They needed to know that there were some dark days, too, as they were sure to have their own tough times. Video of my infamous fall was the perfect footage to portray any embarrassing or disappointing experience they might face in their own lives.

The second part of the event, however, would be my favorite. That's when I could sit down on the floor with the girls around me and have a conversation. The girls could ask me any question they wanted and there would be plenty of time for me to answer. We could also take selfies and do autographs. I loved the idea! The first part would show the gymnasts what was possible, and the second would give them the inspiration to get there. Now when it came time for an autograph, I would know enough about the girl, and have enough time to write something meaningful, rather than just sign my name.

Liz and I spent the entire plane ride excitedly discussing the details and all that it would take to get this idea off the ground. When we got to Florida we continued our brainstorming on the beach, only by now we had moved on to the pitching stage of our idea. We wanted to run the whole thing past my dad, but knew that if he was to embrace the idea, we'd have to have all of the elements logically thought out. So, Liz and I planned, and changed, and planned some more. We even planned the speaking parts of our joint pitch to my dad.

The hard work paid off, because it turned out that our beach time was also excellent preparation for finalizing the details of our new venture in our own minds. Just as I had practiced and rehearsed my skills and routines when I was competing, I found myself following that same concept here. I never wanted to be unprepared, even when my only audience was my mom and dad. We also put our ideas down on paper in a professional format, just as I would if I was pitching something to a professor at NYU, or to a sponsor.

Yes, I was an adult, but I still ran all of the important decisions in my life by both of my parents, because I respect their ideas, knowledge, and experience. I doubt that there will ever come a day when I don't do that; I trust them that much. I also knew that if I talked about the specifics of the idea in detail with my dad, he and my mom would know that Liz and I were serious about it. My dad has always been brutally honest about my ideas, and when I saw that he loved this one, Liz and I forged ahead.

One of the first decisions we had to make was the question of a name for the tour. After some thought, Liz and I came up with Shine. Shine means many things, including self-confidence and doing your best. It also means to glow and excel. All of those words can apply to many different aspects of life, and can be relevant in a variety of situations. Plus, I felt the word was very appropriate to my own life. I had lost my shine for a few years, now this new concept of Shine was giving mine back to me.

Since the 2008 Olympics I had visited a number of gyms, and done autograph sessions at most of them. I had kept good records over the years and those gyms became the starting point for booking The Shine Tour events. Liz was a big help with that, and with so many other things. As with any new business, we had to develop a logo and a web site, set up the business and corporate structure, come up with contracts, book travel and hotels, choose which video clips to include and get them edited together, get a photo shoot done, and a host of other minute details that I was very interested in, but didn't currently have time for.

School was still very important to me—especially because I was learning so many things that I knew would be helpful in my future. I also take personal pride in doing well in activities that I decide to do, so I wanted to do well in school, too. All of that took up precious hours.

Why not wait until I was done with school? Good question, and there are many answers. Mostly, however, I knew there were girls out there right now that I needed to see. If I waited a few years, then they might have graduated from high school, or dropped out of gymnastics and moved on. I felt compelled to reach out to these and other girls as soon as I could.

The big difference between The Shine Tour and my earlier visits to gyms around the country, other than the format, was how the business end of it worked for the gyms. As is standard in personal appearances, for the earlier visits the gyms paid an appearance fee to me through my manager. Even though that is accepted practice, it excluded a number of gyms, especially the smaller ones, as they could not afford the fee. But with The Shine Tour, the attendees would contribute, just like a ticket to a concert. Then, we would give 10 percent back to the gym as a thank you for hosting the event at their location. This meant that virtually every gym could afford to book the tour, and that more girls could benefit from the events.

The first ten gym owners who booked a tour date were people I had known for many years. It was gratifying to know that they not only still supported me, but that they felt the Shine concept had value for their gymnasts and their families. As of this writing we are still in our first year, but already have a wait list of gym owners who want the tour to come to them. It really is exciting and validating to develop an idea into something real, put it out there, and have people embrace it.

At each of our stops there are anywhere from fifty to 125 attendees. Any larger than that and I can't make the personal connections with the girls that are so critical. I have spoken a number of times to much larger audiences, crowds of three to five thousand people. While those events were fun, it means much more to me to connect with every person in the room in a smaller setting.

Girls, young women, and sometimes even their moms, make up the vast majority of our Shine audience, although we have also had a few dads attend, too. While The Shine Tour was developed for a female audience, I am always glad to see dads there, too. Those men were probably pushed out of their comfort zone in attending, but their presence speaks volumes about their love for, and support of, their daughters.

One reason I believe The Shine Tour is effective is that I am honest. I tell the girls that at the start of each new semester at school I feel lonely, out of place, and that I don't know anyone. For an Olympian to share what they feel seems to be powerful and empowering. Suddenly the girls in the audience realize they are not the only person who feels that way, and sometimes there is important dialogue about feelings that starts during our floor time.

When I tell them that I have gotten embarrassed more times than I can count and that my life is not perfect, by any means, people are surprised. That's because they don't know who I am behind the pink leotard and the gold medal. The main message of the tour is that everyone fails in something at some point in his or her life. Me included. So what are you going to do about it? Just lie there? Or, will you pull yourself up and keep going? No matter the size or the circumstance of the fail, you have a decision to make. Hopefully the decision you make will be one that you will still be proud of twenty—or even forty—years from now. Shine is all about life, and the decisions people make when opportunities and challenges arise.

I also share other private feelings of mine, my issues with body image when I was younger, and how all I wanted (other than to get to the Olympics) was to fit in and be just like everyone else. Yes, I agree that being like everyone else and being an Olympian are often two different things, but everyone should dream big, and everyone should feel like they fit in somewhere.

Liz has always been there for me, throughout good times and bad, as were my parents and everyone at WOGA. When I talk about surrounding yourself with good people, I am sure to connect with everyone in the room. So often we make mistakes with our friendships. I want to hammer home the importance of finding people who lift you up and support you. People who make you feel bad about yourself, or who get you in trouble, need to be removed from your life.

If I had any doubt that what I was doing was important, my fears were put to rest during one of our very first tour stops. After the event a mom came up to me with her tall, dark-haired daughter. The girl was sixteen or seventeen, and so beautiful. I realized that she and her mom had been crying.

I looked at them both before the mom started to speak. "Before we came here today, Sarah (name changed) did not believe she was pretty, and didn't believe in herself."

Before her mother could say more, Sarah jumped in. "But I do now," she said, smiling. "What I heard you say makes me believe in me."

Her words gave me goose bumps. I'm not sure what specific words of mine gave Sarah the strength and courage to believe in herself, but I was thrilled that whatever I said made a difference. I had told all of the girls that we are all different and beautiful, and that makes us unique. I also said that most of us put up our best face on social media. We post our happiest moments and our greatest looking photos on Facebook, Twitter, and Instagram, so that's the glimpse of our lives that the world sees. People don't see pictures of us on social media on our bad days, those days where our hair is a mess and we're tired and somehow a big, ugly splotch has gotten on our outfit. Another person's life is not always as glamorous or as fun in reality as it looks online.

I was so fortunate not to have any social media when I was growing up. I can look at social media pages now and understand how people think I have this perfect life, but that is definitely not the case. I have bad days just like everyone else does.

Online, most of us do not show the rest of the world our real selves. We only show the best part of us, so you should not strive to fit in with the perfection that people portray—because it doesn't always exist. Everyone has to have bad days to enjoy the good ones.

I was even more excited because the way Sarah felt had nothing to do with gymnastics. Here was a young woman who lacked self-confidence. That was also true of thousands of girls across the country, boys and young men, too. Turning Sarah's belief in herself into something strong would help her in her school, and her personal and business life, far into the future. It might even help her future children and grandchildren. I left that event feeling so pumped. I had made a difference!

After another, more recent, Shine Tour stop, I received a message from a young woman, a college student who had attended. She was not a gymnast, and never had been, but was a fan of the sport and had rooted for me during the 2008 Games. In short, she told me that she, too, had felt awkward in her own body for many years. She was a girl who had been picked on in school, and like me, also had a "lost" period. Hers was right after high school. Then, for a variety of reasons, she had also encountered a number of disappointments and obstacles in heading toward her top career choice.

The Shine Tour, she wrote, taught her that she had no control over what other people said, felt, thought, or did. The only thing she could control was how she reacted. She now felt strong and capable, and thanked me for being such an inspiration to her. Wow.

Those incidents, along with several others, made me realize that it does not have to take much to turn negative thinking into positive thoughts. It's a kind word, a willingness to share your own experiences, or giving people a sense that even though life has sometimes been hard, you have persevered and come through smiling. That is all it is. The take-away for these two young women, and for everyone, was that if Nastia Liukin could work through difficult days, then they could, too.

I also try to give every person in the audience a sense of his or her own specialness. We are all different, and not everyone is going to win a gold medal at the Olympics, much less even get there, but that's okay. Every person has unique talents and is extraordinary in her own way. How those talents are developed and integrated into life is what is important.

So far we've done about thirty dates, with more being added all the time. Between the broadcasting, school—and all of my ongoing projects with sponsors, USA Gymnastics, and the Olympics—I am busier than ever. But nothing is more important to me than seeing the shine come out in a young girl's eyes. I hope I'll be doing this tour for many years to come.

⁕

As if I didn't have enough on my plate, another opportunity came to me early in 2015. I knew it would be a huge drain on my time, and that it would be one of the hardest things I had ever done. By now you've figured out that I am always up for a challenge, so I discussed the opportunity with my family, Liz, and a few other close friends.

Most people are familiar with *Dancing with the Stars* (DWTS), but in case you haven't watched ABC's popular dance competition, it pairs celebrities with professional dancers. When I was asked to be on the show, I was excited about the idea of doing it, but hesitated. Before the Olympics, and during my competitive career, I had been offered my own reality show no fewer than three different times. Without much discussion, my family and I always said no.

My goal at that time had been to reach the Olympics and we all felt that the distraction of having cameras and a camera crew around all the time would get in the way of my goal. We also did not want the intense media attention that a reality show like that would bring. Media can have a way of distracting you from your true focus and I did not want to get caught up in all of that during that important time in my life.

I also knew that producers of reality television have goals, too. Their main goals are to produce fascinating television and to create programs that lots of people want to watch. Through careful editing, a three-hour training session can be boiled down to thirty seconds and the end result might not necessarily present an accurate tone or focus of the entire session. Even in a reality show about me, we'd have no control over any of that. Then the media could circle back around and jump on the distorted presentation. In the middle of all of that distraction, my goal of becoming an Olympic champion could have been lost.

I still feel that saying no to the idea of reality television was the right thing for me then. But now . . . now might be a different story, especially as this show was a completely different format from what we had discussed before. In talking to my dad, he reminded me that all of the drama that surrounds a show like *Dancing with the Stars* might distract me from school and my other commitments. He did not want to see me become too stressed. He had a valid point. I was very busy. My mom also had the same concerns, but admitted that she would love the pleasure of seeing me perform again.

Along those lines, in the years since my fall at the 2012 Olympic Trials, I had realized something else about myself, something important. I wasn't quite finished with either competing or performing. I missed training seven hours a day, and missed being sore and exhausted most of the time. I even missed the rush of excitement that this kind of a physical goal provided, along with the fulfilling reward of performing a difficult routine well. *Dancing with the Stars* offered me a chance for all of that.

The show also intrigued me because I had always wanted to learn how to dance. Actually, if I had not been a gymnast I think I would have been a dancer. And while my gymnastic floor and beam routines might have incorporated a few easy dance moves, it wasn't quite the same thing as getting through an entire ballroom-style dance.

With all that in mind, the kicker was that I only had a few hours to decide whether or not to do the show. If I accepted, I'd be on *Good Morning America* in three days. So, I thought about it, and decided to say yes.

Chapter Thirteen

One reason I agreed to do the twentieth season of *Dancing with the Stars* was that I was going to be partnered with Derek Hough. In addition to being a professional dancer, Derek is a great choreographer, actor, singer, and songwriter. He, along with his various celebrity dancing partners, have won the coveted DWTS "mirror ball" trophy five times, more than any other pro dancer on the show. He has also won two Primetime Emmy Awards for Outstanding Choreography for routines that he choreographed for the show. Derek turned out to be one of the most talented people I have ever met and obviously, I was in very good hands.

The show airs weekly and is judged by a panel of experts. During the season I was on, the judges were Len Goodman, Julianne Hough, Carrie Ann Inaba, and Bruno Tonioli. In each show, the judges' scores are combined with votes from viewers, and the couple with the lowest combined score is eliminated from the competition. Derek and I hoped that our combined fan base would carry us through as far as my dancing would take us. At the very least, I hoped not to embarrass myself, but that was a risk I was willing to take.

The experience turned out to be filled with expected and unexpected challenges, and I rose to meet each one as gracefully as I could. Some challenges were harder to overcome than others. But I am so glad I was able to test myself through this competition, and I do not regret a single moment spent in rehearsal or in the ballroom.

As my dad had pointed out, if I was going to do the show, the biggest hurdle I had to get past was my commitment to my education. I was still in school and did not want to drop out of a semester I had already committed to. When I heard that Derek was starring in a Radio City Music Hall production, *New York Spring Spectacular: The Rockettes* with Broadway star Laura Benanti, and would be based in New York City during the show, I was thrilled. DWTS is based in Los Angeles, but Derek and I could rehearse between his shows in New York, fly back and forth, and only be in LA for the live shows. It was a plan that worked—for the most part.

Just before all the preparations for the show started, though, I developed a huge case of the jitters and felt so afraid of doing the show that I was almost sick. I was so nervous, in fact, that I almost changed my mind. Fifteen million people were ready and waiting to see every mistake I made, and I realized I was scared to death to put myself out in the public eye in this new format. Well, the format of the show was new to me, anyway. I was afraid because I had no dance experience. Zero. The entire concept of the show brought me completely out of my comfort zone.

Then I had another thought. I could let these powerful thoughts and feelings keep me from an amazing experience, or I could be bold and brave and go for it. With a conscious effort, I changed all the negative self-talk into positive words inside my head. Those fifteen million people could also be waiting to see me succeed. Going into the competition, I told myself that I had many strengths. I was flexible and coordinated, and I learned fast. I was used to doing routines. I took direction well, and I had a good work/practice ethic. I knew that between school and the show I would have no down time, but when all was said and done, fears and all, I was still in. I wanted to do the show far more than I was afraid of it.

I also thought of all of the times people shy away from an opportunity just because they are afraid to try. It is human nature to want to succeed at all you do, but there is no shame in failing, as long as you tried your best. I tried my best lots of times in gymnastics competitions and did not win. Sometimes I didn't even place. On those days there was someone who out-performed me and I always used that information to motivate me to try even harder the next time.

Other than school, my first challenge directly related to the show popped up right away. I was not used to performing with a partner. In gymnastics, I performed alone, so all of the tiny decisions and adjustments that I made during my competitive routines were solely mine. Now I not only had another person to think about, I had someone else calling most of the shots. Those differences were hard to wrap my head around—at first.

Soon, however, I discovered that I had lucked out and gotten a Rolls Royce in a partner. Derek was amazing. He quickly became a friend and I am happy to say that we stayed in touch after Season 20 ended. In addition to his incredible skills as a dancer and a choreographer, he helped me with the mental and emotional side of the show. That was a huge gift. And, from the beginning I trusted him. He is a true professional who has inspired me on so many levels. He also helped me pace myself, and in rehearsal, seemed to know when I had done all I could do for the day.

In addition to everything else, Derek is an excellent teacher who listened to me and validated my thoughts. Even though I wasn't a professional dancer or choreographer, if I mentioned that a move wasn't working for me, he tweaked it so that it did. That alone went a long way toward making me feel comfortable.

Then came another challenge. After we had danced our way through the first week of the show I absolutely was not prepared for the depth of criticism that was directed at me. Throughout my life as a gymnast, I was taught and trained to perform with perfection. I was not encouraged to show emotion during my performance, and in fact, any emotion at all was discouraged. In gymnastics, it is all about the perfection of the skill, and gymnasts are trained to perform with no facial expression.

Dance, I found, was an entirely different story. Dancers need to project the emotion of the music and the movement through their bodies and the expression of their faces. They need to become the role they are dancing and I struggled a lot with this. It was a very difficult transition, because it was hard for me to undo nearly twenty years of training to now do the exact opposite. I was "too much of a gymnast," and I was criticized for this over and over by judges and fans alike.

After the Olympics, there was a lot of media and public attention directed toward me, but it was mostly positive. With *Dancing with the Stars*, not so much. I tried to follow my dad's advice from so long ago and not to read or listen to negative fan comments or media stories. I was far more concerned with what the judges had to say, and Derek and I worked every week to integrate their comments into our next performance. There are a lot of haters and trolls out there on the Internet, but I knew I couldn't be concerned with them. Instead, I had to focus on Derek's and my next dance.

The technique side of the competition was easier for me. As I had hoped, the flexibility and coordination that I had developed during my competitive years helped me out. I picked up most of the dance moves quickly and remembered the routines. My level of fitness ensured that I could still train six to eight hours a day, so we were able to get a lot done.

It helped that my parents flew out each week for the live airing of the show. The producers had offered me a choice between a small apartment and a two-bedroom hotel suite in LA, and I chose the apartment. With my parents (and sometimes my friends and grandparents) regularly coming in, it was a place where we could all be more comfortable. As I typically flew in on a Friday, the apartment also allowed us to have some family dinners, something we had not done much of since I had moved to New York. Those dinners were wonderful. I had missed them far more than I had realized.

One of the many things I loved about being on the show were the many unique costumes that I got to wear. I love fashion, so I had a lot of fun talking with Derek and the designers in the wardrobe department, and working with them to come up with different looks. This was harder than you might imagine, as the costume not only had to fit the theme of the week, the style of the dance, and the specific song, it also had to be comfortable enough to allow me to move my body throughout the dance. Derek's lifetime of experience in the dance world, along with his years on the show, ensured that he had a lot of great costume ideas, and that helped a lot.

In designing the costumes with the creative team, the most important thing to me was that I wore something that really represented me, especially as I have many younger fans, along with my corporate sponsors. I never wanted to look back years from now and think, I wish I had not worn that. After all, I hope my future kids will watch some of my dances one day and I would want them to be proud of me. Fortunately, everyone involved was a pro and knew how to bring Derek's and my ideas to life.

Learning to dance aside, an unanticipated fashion challenge was learning to dance in high heels. When I performed as a gymnast, I was always barefoot. I had worn high heels before, of course, but mostly at red carpet events. Definitely not on the dance floor. But, practice and determination make perfect, and eventually I got the hang of it. Well, most of the time.

The music we danced to each week was integral to the story we were trying to tell, and it turned out to be either a blessing or a curse. Sometimes Derek and I got to choose the music, and I really enjoyed throwing out song ideas and brainstorming. Other weeks, producers chose the music for us. I usually liked the chosen music and could get into the rhythm of it very easily, but there were a few weeks there that were more of a challenge.

Show days were the toughest. As Derek had several shows in New York over the weekend, I would have flown in on Friday to practice the dances with another dancer. Then Derek caught an overnight flight and arrived in LA early on Monday morning. We were on set, rehearsing by seven in the morning and it was a full day of hair, make-up, and more rehearsals. Sometimes there would be last minute changes to a routine, such as the rumba we danced to "Thinking Out Loud." At the last possible moment, we changed the last ten seconds of that dance, and I was so afraid that I wouldn't remember the changes. But I did. That was another high-five moment.

Each week after a show ended, we immediately began getting ready for the next dance. Actually, by Thursday, we had to have the entire dance blocked and on tape to send to the producers, so that was the dance and those were the moves that were solidified in my mind. When changes to the initial routine came along, it always was hard for me to switch gears.

One reason that kind of change always threw me for a loop was that I was used to having years to practice and perfect a routine. Now I only had a matter of days. But, that is part of life, being flexible when you need to be, and stepping up as a team player to perfect last-minute modifications. Even so, it was a huge challenge for me.

As the weeks went on, I still struggled to show enough emotion. Again and again I was criticized for being too technical, and for not having enough soul. I was slowly getting better with this, but I wished the judges and the viewers at home knew how hard I was trying.

Derek and I also had a few challenges that the other competitors did not have. The first was our location. While it worked out most of the time for us to train in New York, there were a few drawbacks. The first was getting on the plane and flying across the country immediately after the show. As soon as the closing credits wrapped, Liz and I made a mad dash for the stage door, and for the car that was waiting for us. Liz would have all my things packed and ready to go, and we'd race to the airport. Sometimes Derek came with us, although he usually flew on a different airline. While I had taken time to change clothes, I typically went through the security checkpoint in full hair and make-up, shedding bobby pins as we ran to catch the plane.

I can't imagine what the other travelers thought. I must have looked ridiculous, but we never missed a flight. That was important, because we were always booked on the last flight out of Los Angeles that flew into New York. It was a red-eye that landed at seven the next morning and my first class at NYU was at nine.

When we got on the plane I'd turn to Liz, who carefully picked her way through the hundred-plus bobby pins that held my numerous hairpieces in place. Once all the extra hair had been removed, I'd wash off whatever make-up was still on, sleep, and study. Had to keep those grades up! The show also didn't help much in my efforts to fit in at school, to be normal, as I got all kinds of stares on campus. Several times I even got a confused, "Didn't I just see you on television last night?"

The other problem with us training in New York was that I did not get to know as many of the other dancers and celebrities as I would have liked. Many of the couples who trained in Los Angeles would bump into each other in the hallway between rehearsals, or they'd all take a lunch break together and hang out, but we did not have that opportunity.

We had a lot of wonderful celebrity dancers my season. Rumor Willis, who won, was absolutely amazing. Willow Shields from *The Hunger Games* is a bright, young star, and I believe we will see a lot more from her. Noah Galloway, the army veteran and amputee was so inspiring. Patti LaBelle, the queen of R&B was there too, as was Riker Lynch, who has a band called R5 with his siblings and also is also a cousin of Derek and Julianne's. Sometimes when you take one opportunity, you have to miss out on another. For me to do *Dancing with the Stars* at all that season, I needed to be in New York. Sadly, the loss of getting to know these and all of my other competitors is mine.

I also felt bad on weeks when we had group or team dances. Whoever was on my team had to work around Derek and me. We could do a lot by Skype, and Derek did what he could to be sure we were on top of all the changes that went on as the choreography progressed in Los Angeles with our team routine, but there is nothing like being in the same room and dancing on the same floor as everyone else. We were able to hold our own, though, even with the handicap of distance.

Any athletic adventure involves some risk, even for seasoned pros like Derek Hough. During Week 7, when Derek was rehearsing with former partner Maria Menounos for an anniversary special, he accidentally kicked a stage light and broke a toe. To make matters worse, when he went down a set of stairs to get ice for his toe, he rolled his ankle and sprained it. Although in the big scheme of things it was a minor injury, it seemed like it would be a season-ending one for Derek, as it happened just before the final weeks of the show.

One reason the celebrities and pros continue to improve as the show goes on is that they get to know each other on a deeper level. The couples also get used to how each partner moves, and can anticipate where the other person is going to go next, and how he or she is going to get there. By Week 7, more than half of the competitors had been eliminated and the skill level of each of the celebrities was ramping up.

When it became clear that Derek would not be able to dance for the next few weeks, I was devastated. How in the world would I find the level of expertise, and the camaraderie and chemistry that I had with Derek with another partner? How could we possibly become a team in just a few short days, especially with me in New York? Enter Sasha Farber.

Like me, Sasha was born in Russia, but he grew up in Australia. He was also a featured dancer in the closing ceremonies of the 2000 Olympic Games in Sydney. As you might guess, we had a few things in common. With Derek overseeing choreography and technique from the sidelines, he came up with a unique trio dance where he, Sasha, and I were sitting on a subway with a few other people (dancers). In the dance routine, Derek gets up to try to dance with me, then waves his hand and sits back down while Sasha and I do a modern Charleston. It seemed to work, and the judges thought so too, as we received the highest score of the night.

The next week had me bouncing between two different settings, one with Sasha and one with Derek. Derek sat for most of his part of the dance, but that worked, too. Another thing that worked was the extra downtime that Derek had after his injury. Since he also could not dance in the Radio City Music Hall show, he and I got to spend more time together. That extra time helped solidify our bond and is one reason the trio dances went so well, as Derek's hand was also in the music and costuming for those dances, as well as the choreography.

Another difficulty for me was the cameras. There was never a time when Derek and I were rehearsing that a camera wasn't pointed at us. I was used to training more privately, without being mic'd and without a group of people following my every move. Here, nothing was off limits. Successes and stresses alike were recorded and we never knew until the last minute what the producers might choose to air on the show.

Plus, some of the producers fed us questions in such a way that I knew they were trying to get Derek or me to answer a certain way. I do not fault them for this, though. The staff at DWTS knew exactly what they needed to produce a top show. That's why it has consistently been in the top ratings for more than ten years.

Odd questions were also thrown at me a few times after the performance, when host Erin Andrews or Tom Bergeron asked a question that I hadn't thought about. People who live in the spotlight far more than I do might have been better at this than I was, but when I was exhausted from a demanding routine, and nervous about my score and from being on live television, I think I could have done better with some of my answers. It can also be very loud in the ballroom and sometimes it is hard to hear what is being asked. In viewing other DWTS contestants, though, it seemed they had the same issue with these things that I had. However, it usually makes for good television!

One other thing that didn't work so well, at least from Derek's and my viewpoint was a package (a short video segment) that was shown just before a jive that I did with Derek and Sasha. The package showed us getting frustrated, then a producer asked me a question that had nothing to do with the show or what we were doing. Were we frustrated and exhausted at times? Of course. We had just worked hard for eight hours, and with Derek's injury it was definitely a challenge. But we *never* had an argument, and that is what they tried to make out of it.

The resulting package was shown live to the viewers and everyone in the ballroom just before we did our jive. We had not seen it before and I was very disappointed in it, as I looked like a spoiled brat. Ironically, the other six days we rehearsed we were laughing and smiling all the time, but they didn't show any of that. Derek was not pleased with the package either, but we had to swallow our feelings and go out there and perform. That was hard, but we both were professionals so we sucked it up and did our best.

The main reason for my disappointment was that I had tried very hard to show the real me throughout the show, and that package was not who I was. They took a single thirty-second segment out of an entire week and made me look like something I was not.

Then there was the scoring process. In gymnastics, it was all about the judges' scores. Whatever they scored showed up on the leader board and that score determined who won a particular event. Not so here. The viewer voting component could throw the judges' scores completely out of whack. Good judges scores were needed for sure, but a competitor also needed strong votes from the viewers. The uncertainty was hard, but at least every couple in the ballroom was dealing with the same situation, and the same feelings.

Despite the many challenges I loved being on the show, and it was upsetting was when Derek and I were eliminated in the semi-finals. We'd had the top score the week before, but were prepared for the fact that we might leave, as several excellent dancers had left in the weeks before I did. I packed a dress, just in case. The eliminated couple was always on *Good Morning America* the next morning and I wanted to be sure I had something to wear—if I needed it. I could come back to the apartment at a later date, to pack everything up.

It turned out that I did need the dress, and Derek and I flew back to New York that night. I steamed the wrinkles out of my dress just moments before we went live on the air. We were both so tired by the time the *Good Morning America* cameras turned their lenses toward us that it seemed like we were holding each other up. In addition to the all-night flight, we'd been running on adrenaline for the past nine weeks. Between Derek's show, my classes, and all the media and other public appearances in between, we were both exhausted. Now that the pressure was off, now that we were no longer in the competition, it was as if all the adrenaline whooshed right out of us and left us feeling flat.

That GMA appearance was bittersweet. I admit that I like to win, but even though I didn't take home the mirror ball trophy, the entire *Dancing with the Stars* experience made me feel like a winner. I did so many things that were out of my comfort zone. I also met a number of incredible people, and even learned to dance some along the way. Without a doubt, I know I will always be glad that I put my fears aside to go on this incredible journey.

Chapter Fourteen

*B*ecause of my single focus on the Olympics during my teen years, I didn't really start dating until after the 2008 Games. Early in my dating life, it seemed that everyone I wanted to go out with lived on the other side of the country. Either that, or they traveled as much as I did. It always is hard to make a long-distance relationship work, and over time, my long-distance relationships fizzled out, too.

Jumping into the challenging new world of dating was another big transition for me, mostly because I was so far behind the rest of my peers in this area. Dating creates opportunities to learn important social skills, but I was busy trying to get to the Olympics when other kids my age were getting to know each other. I would not have had it any other way, but it certainly was a trade off.

Now, when I met someone I thought I'd like to know better, I had no idea what to say. I became tongue-tied. I wasn't really that socially inept, but I got so excited about the possibility of going out on a date that I became a little giddy.

Of course, I made the usual mistakes and dated a few people who were totally unsuited. There are many men and women out there who are just looking to have fun. There is nothing wrong with that; it is just the stage of life they are in. I must have completely skipped over that stage, however, because when it came to dating, from day one I was looking for more. I wanted a solid relationship; one just like my parents had. I was looking for long-term.

Finding the person you might spend the rest of your life with takes time. Two parents who still loved each other raised me, and there were many good guys in my life who were coaches or family friends. I knew good guys existed, and did not want to settle for anything less. If my standards meant going on fewer dates, well, that was fine with me. I didn't want to waste time—either my date's or mine.

Over the years I dated a few guys who were fun, interesting, and potential husband material, but for one reason or another, those relationships were not meant to be. By the summer of 2014, I had only brought one boy home for my parents to meet. Then for various reasons that relationship ended too.

One day in the summer of 2014 I attended the engagement party of a friend in New York, and my life changed forever. I was standing in a group of people, talking, and one of them was a guy named Matt Lombardi. Matt, I gathered, was from Boston, and was a former hockey player for Boston College. He'd played professional hockey for several years but had recently moved on and co-founded a mobile technology company that is transforming coaching with a first-of-its kind mobile platform called Drivn. And that was it. That was all I knew. Except that before I left, he said, "If you're ever in Boston, call me." Then we went our separate ways without even exchanging phone numbers.

There was something about Matt that I liked on first sight. Of course, he was tall, dark, and handsome, but there was also something about him that intrigued me—along with a sense that he was a good guy. A really good guy.

I couldn't stop thinking about him, so the next day I friended Matt on Facebook and was thrilled, when he texted me shortly after that. A mutual friend had given him my phone number.

After that, for the next few days we called or texted each other constantly. I remember texting until three AM, then getting up exhausted but so energized and excited, at six AM for class, and starting the constant texting and talking all over again. For a number of days, neither of us got much sleep.

That's what it is like at the beginning of a relationship, but that intensity is not necessarily a bad thing as it allows each party to spot major red flags in the other's personality, belief system, and life plans. I did not run across anything Matt said that let me believe that he was anything less than perfect for me. If I had, however, I hope I would have been smart enough to put the brakes on the budding relationship until I could think through whatever might have bothered me about him. Too often I had seen friends who ignored early warning signs and found themselves in a very bad relationship later on.

The very next weekend Matt came to town and we spent the whole weekend doing touristy things. It was great, because Matt had not spent a lot of time in New York City, and while I had been here for a while, I had not had time to see some of the best parts of the city. We ate at a sushi restaurant and visited Freedom Tower, the inspiring World Trade Center memorial. Then we took a romantic walk through Central Park. The entire weekend was wonderful!

The next weekend I went to Boston and Liz insisted on coming with me. As my best friend, she wanted to meet this person I thought so much of. Everyone should have a friend who cares about them as much as Liz cares about me. Liz and I drove to Boston together and I was thrilled to find that she not only approved of Matt, she genuinely liked him. He clinched the deal, though when he took us to dinner and had country music playing on the radio. Country was Liz's favorite.

During one of our first dates, I learned that one of Matt's friends had told him that I was a gymnast, and that I had won a gold medal at the Olympics. Matt was proud of my accomplishment, but seemed far more interested in what I was doing now, and in my plans for the future. That was a huge wake up call for me about this relationship. Usually when I met people, the Olympics came up right away and we never moved beyond that. Every conversation then revolved around what I had done back in 2008. Honestly, that is the last topic I want to talk about when I am getting to know someone and it usually is very awkward for me to try to move the conversation on to something else.

Don't get me wrong. I am extraordinarily proud of what I achieved, and of my ongoing involvement with USA Gymnastics and the Olympics. It's just that I am more than that, more than a gold medal. Matt and I discussed the Olympics once, and together we watched the DVD of my routines from the 2008 Beijing Games. Then he asked a few questions and that was it.

We spent most of our early dates getting to know each other as we are now, rather than who we had been six years earlier. I also liked that Matt supported all that I was doing with the different projects I was involved in. He, too, was an entrepreneur, and like many who start new ventures, he did not have a typical nine-to-five job. His work was done when it needed to be, whether that was at nine AM or nine PM. My life was a lot like that, too, so we really understood each other on many different levels, and in many different areas.

Within a month I began to feel that Matt might be "the one." I had never felt as comfortable or as safe around anyone as I did him, and I also had not loved anyone as much or had as much fun with anyone as I did with him. I realize that one month is quite early in a relationship to feel so strongly, but as I got to know him, I realized that Matt and I are very similar as people. He was thoughtful and steady and fun. And, we both came from close families. The only big difference was that Matt had two older sisters and I am an only child. I still wanted Matt to meet my parents, and for his parents to meet them, too. I was so happy when that happened, because everyone got along really well.

When two people are in a relationship and thinking about marriage, they often do not think about the family of the person they love. I have always believed that if you marry someone, you marry his or her family, too. You marry their background, culture, traditions, siblings, and parents. If you do not think of those things going in, then they are likely to cause problems within the marriage at some later date.

Throughout the fall of 2014 and into the early months of 2015, Matt and I began to realize that we wanted to be together for the rest of our lives. Neither of us was ready for more than that mutual understanding, but it was a steady and comforting feeling to know that he'd always have my back, and I his.

When *Dancing with the Stars* came along, Matt was in the audience almost every week. I, of course, had run that opportunity by Liz and my parents, but this was the first time I had also included Matt in a big career decision. He had actually been sitting on the couch with me in my apartment in New York when my agent at the time called with the offer from the producers of the show, so he was one of the first people I talked to about it. I was especially sensitive to the fact that Matt might be uncomfortable with me working so closely with Derek, but Matt was totally supportive of this opportunity for me.

On Monday, June 1, 2015, a few weeks after my season on *Dancing with the Stars* ended, Matt and I were in Boston and were scheduled to go to dinner with a friend—or so I thought. Before we left, he asked me to look in my bag, to see if his wallet was there. I looked, and in my bag I saw the most gorgeous engagement ring. I wasn't sure if I was supposed to have seen it though, so I turned back to Matt, and there he was, down on one knee.

"Are we really going to dinner with a friend?" I asked.

"No," he said, smiling, "we are going out to celebrate."

Of course I said yes—to the celebration and the proposal. I was so excited! I was getting married to the love of my life! I began to text my friends, his friends, my family, and his family. I desperately wanted to share our good news, but no one texted me back. I even tried to FaceTime with Liz on my phone, but Matt pressed the end call button. "Let's just enjoy this evening at the restaurant, just the two of us," he said.

Even though I wanted to share, I was fine with that as nothing could spoil my excitement. *Everyone will get back to me soon,* I thought. In the meantime, I wanted to enjoy my newly engaged status, and admire the amazing ring that Matt had designed especially for me.

Imagine my shock and surprise when Matt and I got to the restaurant to find my parents, Matt's family, Liz, and Matt's best friend Ben Smith—all the people who were ignoring my texts and calls—waiting for us at the restaurant. My parents had flown in from Dallas, Liz from New Orleans, and Ben from Connecticut, all to be there for us. Matt had arranged it all, coordinated everyone's schedule, and had managed to keep it all a secret!

Later, I found out that a month earlier Matt had asked my dad if he could marry me. They had both been in Los Angeles to see me on *Dancing with the Stars*, and had gone to breakfast together. Matt said he wanted to ask my dad a question, and my dad later told me that he thought he knew what might be coming. He and everyone else could see how much in love Matt and I were. When Matt told my dad that I was the best thing that had ever happened to him and that I made his life better each and every day, what could my dad do but agree?

From day one Matt has been nothing but a gracious, caring, loving gentleman when it comes to my family, and I was so glad that he did everything the old-fashioned way. Asking my dad before he asked me was a huge sign of respect. And, because of the respect he showed my parents in asking, it further united our two families. I still don't know how everyone kept this huge, wonderful secret from me for four entire weeks!

Between graduating from NYU and my duties with NBC, USA Gymnastics, and my sponsors, I have a pretty packed schedule with events leading up to and including the 2016 Olympic Games. It will be a very exciting but busy time for me on the Road to Rio, which is why we plan to get married in June of 2017. Matt and I both want to have a big wedding, and that takes a lot of planning. I didn't want my professional career to interfere with the biggest day of my life, but after the Olympics I will still have plenty of time to attend to all the details a bride needs to. Matt and I are in no hurry. We know we will be together forever.

Initially, I had planned to return to Dallas after I had graduated from college to be closer to my parents, and because Dallas is "home." But Matt's new business venture and his team are all based in Boston, so after graduation, I will be moving there. It would not be fair of me to ask Matt to relocate when all of his business interests are settled in Boston. Maybe someday my mom and dad will move closer to us, or maybe Matt's company will open a Dallas branch. Who knows what the future will bring?

Matt has always supported me in my career decisions, and that is so important in a life partner. And, I have supported his. I see so many couples who are torn apart by a lack of mutual support. If one partner does not fully support the hopes, goals, and dreams of the other, then the marriage will suffer. Often, it does not survive.

I waited twenty-five years to find the perfect person for me, and I am so happy that I waited until Matt came along. Everyone needs someone who treasures them just for who they are. And if I can find someone who not only puts up with my crazy schedule and my big hopes and dreams, but also actively supports all of that, then anyone else can find that too.

I don't know what challenges life will throw at Matt and me down the road, either individually or as a couple. I do know that whatever they are, they will be easier to face with a loving, supportive partner at my side. I can't wait!

Chapter Fifteen

For a few years now, I have wanted to write a book like this, not to share all of my successes in life, but to let readers know that I, too, have faced many disappointments. Over the years so many people told me I couldn't write a book. They told me there was nothing interesting about my life, and that no one would be intrigued by my story. So I accepted their challenge and took it upon myself to prove them wrong. I felt I had a lot to share and wanted to write a book that would let readers know that everyone has ups and downs. With any triumph comes setbacks, and it is important for everyone to know that even Olympic champions need to find motivation wherever, and whenever, they can.

Whether it is in sports or in life, many goals are hard to reach. I know that the road to my goal of medaling at the Olympics was incredibly long and tough. That's why I want to share my motivation techniques here, in hopes that they might help you as they have helped me.

First, you must decide what your goal is. Your goal could be sports related, or it could involve business, academics, family, friends, a special skill, or a social cause. This works not just for long-term goals, but short-term goals as well. My parents always taught me to have daily, weekly, and monthly goals. Finding your goal is easier said than done for some people, me included. I have so many things I am doing now and want to do soon, that I have to prioritize, even though I am excited about each and every project.

It is important that you personally commit to your goal. Make a pact with yourself that you will see your dream through to the very end. Then, whenever things get hard, which they inevitably will, you have major incentive to keep going. The one person you do not want to let down is yourself.

At some point you actually have to stop thinking about your goal and get started on the road to achievement. This can be a hard transition. That's why you must pick a start day and map out a plan. When are you going to work on your goal? Will it be every day, three times a week, twice a month? What time during the day? For how long? Make appointments with yourself to work on your dream and be sure not to cancel on yourself. If you do, you will be the one person who is negatively affected.

Getting started can be frightening. In the past I have often thought, *what if I fail?* Well, I have failed. Big time. I fell on my face in front of about twenty-thousand people during a time when both fans and those in the gymnastics world expected much more from me. Trust me, your failure cannot get much more humiliating than that. Whenever I have negative thoughts of failure I turn them around. What if I succeed? What will happen then? What amazing thing can I do after I reach my goal? And remember, my huge, falling "failure" turned out to be one of the most defining moments of my life.

Thinking positive thoughts is key to any success, so make sure that you are consciously aware of your inner self-talk. All of us talk to ourselves, but we are not always aware of our words, so start listening. Would you tell your best friend the negative things you are saying to yourself? Would you say them to your mother? When listening, if you hear negative words in your head, push them out and replace them with positive messages to yourself. Before the start of every routine during a competition I would tell myself,

"Always keep a positive thought, because a positive thought cannot be denied." You will be surprised how this one change in thinking can positively affect every area of your life.

You must also try to work to overcome your fears. There are many more kinds of fears than the specific fear of failure, or public humiliation in not reaching your goal. Depending on your goal, you might have fears of injury, of missing out on other things, of not having the support you need, or of not being up to the challenge. There are hundreds of kinds of fears, but you must take time to identify what yours are and find a way to get past them. You can do that through positive self-talk, by objectively assessing how realistic your fears are, and by breaking the fear into parts to discover which areas of the fear most bother you.

If you have a fear of public speaking for example, and that is a component of your goal of becoming a great teacher, find out what part of speaking to others bothers you most. Is it large crowds? Then start by speaking to very small groups. Is it standing in front of the room with everyone looking at you? Try speaking while sitting on top of a desk. Is it that you are afraid you will forget what you are supposed to say? Then practice so much that you know your material instinctively, inside and out, and can recite it at the drop of a hat.

Know that it is okay to be afraid. Many things worth having are scary to achieve. Those kinds of fears are normal, because it is hard for many of us to move beyond our comfort zone. How you handle your fears, though, that's the important thing. When you finally step up to push your fears away and live the journey of your goal without fear, it is the most empowering thing you can imagine. Only then will life bring you the most amazing experiences. I guarantee that you will not want to miss them.

Keep in mind that I am not talking about doing crazy things here. If your goal is to jump off a thousand-foot cliff without a parachute, that's a goal I would think twice about. If your goal involves being around mean, abusive, or dangerous people, think again. Find a new goal; there are plenty out there. One of them is sure to interest you.

After you have started, it is important to keep your end goal in sight. If you have a big, long-term goal, such as sailing around the world, it is not always easy to remember the big picture, because it is so far away. I always set daily, weekly, and monthly goals, and adjust accordingly as I go along. In working on those smaller goals, I keep in mind the great feeling I will have when my dream has become reality.

Those smaller daily goals are also easier to achieve then your big main goals. Sometimes huge, long-term goals can be over-whelming. Instead of focusing on one huge goal, such as an Olympic medal, I might have focused, for example, on learning one new skill by the end of the month. That way I could incorporate the skill into a new routine that I wanted to do at a specific competition that led to the Olympics. Baby steps are important. They are a critical part of your journey.

The new skill might have been part of my dream of reaching the Olympics, but it also became a sort of mini-goal in and of itself. In learning it, I broke the skill down into parts, mastered each element of the skill, and then put it back together. When I had done all of that and could perform the new skill flawlessly, I felt great! It's hard to maintain one motivation for a single goal for a long period of time, so a good solution is to have many smaller goals along the way. That way you are always achieving and can high-five your way to success.

When I was striving toward my Olympic medals, so many people told me that I couldn't get there. I try not to think what might have happened if I had listened to them. Oh, their words definitely affected me sometimes. Actually, more than just some-times. Those words affected me a lot. On some days it was hard not to sink into a negative way of thinking. Then I remembered that if I worked hard and stayed focused, I had just as good a shot as anyone else. Never let anyone's negative words tear you down. Even if you don't achieve your goal as you first envisioned it, you will have learned a lot about yourself and life along the way, met some great people, and had some interesting experiences. Those are never bad things.

When I was competing, I never envisioned that I would fall during a big competition, but I did. And, in the months and years after that day I learned a surprising thing. I could do many things that did not involve a flip on a balance beam, or a release on the uneven bars. Gymnastics shaped my life, but there was much more in store for me. I believe that concept is true for everyone. That's why we need to be open to the many specific and unexpected gifts that we get on the way to our goal—and be sure to celebrate them.

I mentioned my visualization board before, the board I placed by my window in my room with photos of my goals and my dad's medal hanging from it. Boards like that are great to have, as you can see and focus on the outcome of your dream. You can make your own board out of poster board, a bulletin board, a dry erase board, or anything that will hold visual images of your dream.

Some people also decorate their board with gold stars or motivating quotes or sayings. The beauty of the board is that it is yours. There is no right or wrong. Whatever motivates *you* is what should be on it.

I wasn't always in the same room with my board, however. It wasn't as if I could carry it with me and look at it all day at the gym. That's why I liked to take some quiet time every day to visualize the successful outcome of my goal in great detail. This is easy to do. Just close your eyes, and experience in your mind how your successful outcome will look, feel, smell, taste, and sound. Where are you when you reach your goal? What are you wearing? What is the temperature? What time of day is it? What time of year? Who, if anyone, is with you? Now experience all of these thoughts and feelings in your mind as if you were actually there. This can be done for each of your smaller goals as well.

Skeptical? Numerous university studies have proven the power of visualization as it relates to success. I hope you give it a try. It should be done every day, but it is especially effective for days or times when you cannot work on your goal any other way. Doctors and scientists still do not know a lot about the subconscious mind, but visualization can help your mind acknowledge every step of success, even while you are achieving it.

While visualization is very important, there comes a time when you have to experience in real life, rather than in your head, so work hard at your goal as often as you can. Nothing happens if you do not put forth the energy to get there. For the rest of my days I will be known as an Olympic gymnast, and I am proud of that, but if I want other things to happen I have to put in the time to make them reality, too. Nothing happens without directed and positive effort.

You must also educate yourself about your end goal as much as possible. Learn everything you can about it from people who are in the know. Read every book that every expert has written about your goal—and then learn from their successes and mistakes. Watch all the DVDs and documentaries on the subject that you can. Also, learn about others who have accomplished what you want to, and know who the current leaders in the field are.

If it is helpful to your goal for you to have a coach or trainer, find the best one that you can. If it is a different sort of a goal, find a mentor, an expert advisor who will advise you on the plusses and minuses of each step you take toward reaching your dream. These people, whether coaches or mentors, can help you avoid common pitfalls that might detour you away from your goal. Another brain and another set of eyes helping you toward your goal can get you there faster and more easily than you can on your own.

But it has to be the right set of eyes, and the right brain. If you feel your coach or advisor is not as invested in your goal as he or she should be, look around. Find someone else, or a series of someone else's until the right person falls into place. Sometimes as you progress on the path to your goal, you will outgrow a trusted helper. That's okay. It is a bittersweet sign of progress for sure, but they want you to succeed and surely know their own strengths. They might even help you find the next person who will help you along your journey.

Be sure also to give your dream the time it needs to evolve. It is hard to be patient, especially when so many people today expect quick results. We live in a society that expects instant gratification, and that is not going to happen here. Those smaller goals will keep you moving forward, but you may need to remind yourself daily (hourly if necessary) that your big dream will take time to achieve. In the meantime, be happy with whatever progress you have made so far, and be happy with your ability to stick with your goal.

One thing that will help attract you to success is to find inspiration anywhere you can. This could be a blog, a news story about someone else's success, a kind word from a friend, or the support of a family member. An amazing photograph, a magazine article, book, quote, song, or even people you meet for the first time can inspire you. Nature, in the form of a beautiful spring morning could motivate you, or the happy expression on your dog's face as he greets you at the door. Find inspiration where, how, and whenever you can. If you actively look for it, you will be surprised at how much of it is out there.

You must also have a hero. Just as I had Lilia Podkopayeva, you must have someone to look up to as well. Your hero does not have to be involved in whatever field your goal or dream is in; it could just be an amazing person whom you look up to. If your hero is still living and you haven't already, find a way to meet him or her. Find your hero's good qualities and try to emulate them. But don't expect your hero to be perfect. No one is, and perfection in all areas of a person's being is too much to ask. Besides, imperfection is what makes people interesting.

In addition to believing in your hero, you absolutely must believe in yourself. If you do not believe that you can really, truly achieve your goal, then who else will believe in you? This belief involves making an honest assessment of your strengths and weaknesses, and developing a plan to become even better in your areas of strength, and filling in the gaps of your weaker areas. Visualization and positive self-talk will help you believe deeper than you ever thought possible. Also, when you believe, others will believe, too.

When all is said and done, we all have moments when we want to quit. As my mom often said, "You can quit any time you want, but you can't quit after a bad day. When you quit, quit after a *good* day." That is such important advice and I can't tell you the number of times it has been helpful to me.

One of the most powerful things you can do when you are in the middle of making a dream a reality is to start being more conscious of those times when you become discouraged. Do they come when you are tired, or after you've had a fight with a sibling or a spouse? Try documenting in your phone or tablet, or even in a notebook, all the times during a given week when you are discouraged. Write as much as you can about how you feel and what the circumstances are around your discouragement. Then at the end of the week look at your notes. It may become crystal clear that you have a desire to quit on days when you forgot to eat lunch, after a poor night's sleep, or after talking with a specific person.

Once you know what is causing your thoughts about quitting, you can develop a plan to counteract your feelings. Write down the plan now, because I guarantee that when you feel discouraged, you will not be in the mood to write down a positive plan of action. Your plan might be an easy fix: remember to eat, sleep well, limit your interactions with certain people, or go to a certain visualization in your mind. Harder fixes require more thought, but take the time to come up with a plan. Then you can pull it out when you need it.

Some people find it is helpful to record their thoughts and feelings, and their successes and challenges in reaching their goal, in a daily journal or notebook. This can be a helpful tool, as long as you are honest with yourself. Over time, you can look back into the last week, month, or even year, to see how far you have come. That written validation of your progress might just be the motivation you need to power through another day.

Of course, nothing happens without great time management, and I find that is something a lot of people struggle with. You must create the time to work on your dreams. I keep a copy of my schedule in my phone and in my computer, and find that I get more done if I prioritize, so make a list of the things you have to get done every day in the order of importance. Then tackle the list from the top down. If you find a hole in your schedule, take something from the list and do it right then. Knock it out and cross it off your to do list.

Before I met Matt, I didn't think I had time for a boyfriend. Then I remembered that my dad always said, "Make time for things that matter." Matt mattered to me, so I made time for him. It was as simple as that. I'd often take a four-hour train ride from New York to Boston and then ride back again, all in the same day, just so I could spend a few hours with someone I cared about.

It's a bit ironic, actually. My dad was still training when he was dating my mom, but he made time to drive the two hours each way that it took for him to take her out to dinner. This is not to say that he or I dropped the ball in other areas of our lives. We just rearranged our priorities and our schedules to fit in someone who was important to us.

Time management is important because you will do better in everything you do if you do not scramble to get it done at the last minute. If you have a report due, don't wait until the last minute. Do it now. It will be a much better report if it was not last minute. That's also why I am always on time. Actually, I often am a few minutes early. I am usually the first one in class, and am focused and ready to participate and learn by the time my professor and classmates arrive. Being on time is also a nice courtesy to the people you are meeting. They have things to get done, too, and it is rude and inconsiderate to be dismissive of their time by showing up late.

These ideas, along with others that you will come up with on your own, can help you give 100 percent in all you do. And that is important. I love the feeling of achievement, of success, but it takes organized dedication to get there.

Some of these ideas might be more useful to you than others, but I hope you will try them all to see what works best for you. When you finally achieve your goal, however you got there, you will have the greatest feeling. So be sure to take time to celebrate. You have earned that special time with family and friends. But even more important, you can then find a new goal that will challenge you and expand your horizon even more.

I remember how lost I was after the Olympics, because I didn't know what came next. If you don't have a new goal in mind before you achieve the old, don't worry. Something is sure to come along to pique your interest, and this time, you will have the tools in place to get there. You will have found what practices work best for you and you will be able to enjoy this new journey even more. But most important, don't be afraid to set a goal or a dream that might seem "too big." There's no such thing!

Imagine if everyone was positively working toward great things. What an amazing world this would be.

Chapter Sixteen

$\mathcal{M}$y life so far has definitely been interesting and fun, and while I am excited about the future I am no longer so concerned that every step of it needs to be planned. That's been tough for me, to let go of having my entire life scripted years in advance.

My immediate future involves graduating from college. If formal education is not your best strength, then find another way to continue to learn and to become an expert in an area that you are passionate about. Even after I earn my degree I know that I will never stop learning all I can about things that interest me. Between books, radio programs, podcasts, DVDs, documentaries, lectures, and seminars, there are many ways to continue to learn outside of formal education. But it will be up to you to take the initiative and to absorb the material. I hope you do.

Matt and I will be getting married, and I am looking forward to moving to Boston, decorating our new home, and settling into married life. I am also looking forward to becoming part of his family. I never had siblings, and am excited that his two sisters will also become mine.

We do plan to have kids at some point. I would not want to miss the experience of being a mom, or of Matt and me parenting our children together. Some wonderful day many years from now,

I even hope to be a grandmother. When it comes to our children, Matt and I have already put thought into how we will handle their individual interests. Because I grew up so immersed in gymnastics and Matt grew up so immersed in hockey, we want to be sure that we do as our parents did and only encourage activities that our kids are interested in. If I have a daughter who is passionate about ballet, tennis, volleyball, chess, or biking, then I know I will do everything I can to see that she explores her interests as much as she wants to. Matt feels the same way. However, just as I experimented with piano, each of our kids will probably get an introduction to gymnastics and hockey as part of trying a lot of different things to see where their interests and talents lie.

When I was a child, I pushed myself into gymnastics. No one made me start it, or stay in it, and no one ever forced me to go to the gym. I wanted to experience the sport as far as it would take me, and it was what I wanted to do more than anything else. I just hope that our children find something to be equally as passionate about. Whatever it is, Matt and I will support them in their interests, just as our parents supported us in ours.

Within my own family, my grandparents recently moved from Russia to Dallas and I am thrilled that I will get to see them more, and that they will even get to meet my own children one day. I so valued my relationships with my great-grandparents that I hope my grandparents and my children also can have that kind of a bond. And there is another reason I am glad they will be closer and that I will get to see them more often. I can practice my Russian with them, and maybe can even help them learn more English, just as I helped my parents learn the language so many years ago.

On the career front I hope to continue my broadcasting career with NBC well into the future. I love breaking down gymnastics for the viewers, and as the sport grows, I hope its television coverage also expands. Certainly I will stay involved in USA

Gymnastics, the gymnastics world, and the Olympics, but I am no longer desperate to know exactly how all of that will play out over the coming years. Instead of stressing over every possibility, I can now focus intently on each event, on each opportunity, and take it all step-by-step.

When it comes to Shine, Liz and I will be expanding that brand as well. I am eager to see where Shine goes, because my passion for motivating girls and young women is boundless. We have only touched the surface of what we can do, and thinking of the many possibilities is exciting. One thing at a time, though. As Liz and I want give every project 100 percent, some of our plans will have to stay on the back burner for a while. I have no doubt that as we grow and expand the company, that we will be involved in more events in more cities.

Yes, I am excited about my future, but I am also excited about yours. We live in an amazing time, especially when it comes to women. Every day, we see more women becoming CEOs, judges, doctors, business owners, lawyers, senators and more. We live in a world where women absolutely can succeed. We can be anything we want to be.

I've mentioned passion before, many times in fact. But finding something you are passionate about is an important part of finding your shine. Whether it involves a career, a family, a sport, or a hobby, I know when a person, male or female, young or old, has found their passion and their shine. I know because there is something electric in their being. These are the people who are exciting to be around, and you can see their passion for life shining in their eyes.

That's what I want for you. I want everything for you that you want for yourself, only more. I hope that you will immerse yourself fully in whatever your interests are, and learn all you can about them. Whatever it is that you want to do, short- or long-term, I hope you give it your all. Then, if you decide to switch gears, you can say you pursued your passion as far as you could go. And, you can say that with tremendous pride.

Sometimes girls come up to me and say, "But what if I work hard toward something and decide I don't want to do that anymore?" That's a great question, and of course it is okay to change your passions. If one no longer gives you your shine, then find something else that does. People switch sports, hobbies, and careers all the time. If you don't like what you are doing, then do something else. No matter what you do or have done, you will have learned something that you can draw from at some point in the future.

I love trying new things, and that is what life is about. The last thing I want is for you to think, *I wish I'd tried that.* Try everything that interests you, as long as it is safe. And you know what? It's okay not to like things you think you might have liked. You tried it. Great! Now you know it is not for you, so try something else. Keep trying until you find a sport, event, cause, or subject that really, *really* interests you. Then go for it. There are a lot of things I still want to try during my lifetime, and eventually I believe I will get to them all.

When it comes to your goals, know that you don't have to be successful at everything. Not every day needs to end with an Olympic medal hanging around your neck. It's okay to not reach your goal, as long as you either had fun in the process or learned something—and in every experience there is always something important to learn.

My challenge to you is to live life fully. Don't let anyone or anything hold you back from your dreams. Know that you can be anything, anyone, you choose to be, but that to get there involves some hard work. Don't give up just because the going gets tough. The end result will be worth everything you put into it, and more.

I hope my words have been helpful to you. If so, think about sending me a message through my social media. You can find those links in the Resources section at the end of this book. I'd love to hear from you, and about all of your successes. I also hope to meet you at a Shine Tour stop or other event down the road.

As we go forward into our futures, I hope you will keep one last thought in mind. You are special, you are unique, and you are beautiful inside and out. Now, go find your shine.

About the Author

orn in Moscow, Russia, Nastia moved to the United States with her parents when she was two and a half. As the daughter of two champion gymnasts, it was only natural that Nastia found herself in the gym at a very young age. Nastia began competing at the age of six, and by the time she was twelve was an elite gymnast.

Despite several debilitating physical injuries, Nastia won nine world championship medals (four gold and five silver) and five Olympic medals (one gold, three silver, and one bronze), making her one of the most celebrated gymnasts in US history and only the third American woman in history to win the Olympic all-around title.

Nastia headlined the 2012 Kellogg's Tour of Gymnastics Champions, and in January 2013 began college at NYU where she is studying sports management. Nastia works as a television commentator for various events, including the USA Nationals Championships, World Championships and the upcoming 2016 Olympic Games. She was a special correspondent for NBC at the 2014 Olympic Winter Games in Sochi, Russia.

Outside of gymnastics, Nastia has modeled for BCBG/Max Azria, teamed up with Fisher-Price to introduce a new interactive Dora the Explorer doll, launched a line of signature clothing at

JCPenny called Supergirl by Nastia, and also has her own signature lines of equipment with AAI, and gymnastics apparel with GK Elite Sportswear.

Nastia also created The Shine Tour, a motivational and inspirational event for girls and young women. The tour is a chance for Nastia to interact with girls of all ages—athletes and non-athletes—to share her story and talk with them about issues they are facing. Her hope is that every person in the audience will leave feeling inspired to shine in her own life.

In early 2015 Nastia was a contestant on *Dancing with the Stars* and was partnered with pro dancer Derek Hough. The couple was eliminated in the semi-finals, despite having had a perfect score the week before. Nastia is fluent in both English and Russian and has a strong interest in fashion, education, and philanthropy. She lives in Dallas, Boston, and New York City, and can be reached at info@shineagency.com.

Resources

Nastia Liukin
Email: info@shineagency.com
Facebook: facebook.com/NastiaLiukin08
Instagram: instagram.com/nastialiukin
Pinterest: pinterest.com/nastialiukin/
Twitter: @NastiaLiukin
Website: nastialiukin.com

The Shine Tour
Website: theshinetour.org

The Shine Agency
Email: info@shineagency.com
Twitter: @Shine_Agency
Website: shineagency.com

WOGA
Facebook: facebook.com/WOGA-Gymnastics-145725238779846
Instagram: instagram.com/wogagymnastics
Twitter: @wogagymnastics
Website: woga.net

USA Gymnastics

Facebook: facebook.com/USAGymnastics

Instagram: instagram.com/usagymnastics Twitter: @USAGym

Website: usagym.org

The Olympic Games

Facebook: facebook.com/olympics

Instagram: instagram.com/olympics

Twitter: @Olympics

Website: olympic.org

New York University

Facebook: facebook.com/NYU

Instagram: instagram.com/nyuniversity

Twitter: @nyuniversity

Website: nyu.edu

Dancing with the Stars

Facebook: facebook.com/dancingwiththestars

Instagram: instagram.com/dancingabc

Pinterest: pinterest.com/DancingABC

Twitter: @DancingABC

Website: abc.go.com/shows/dancing-with-the-stars

Nastia Liukin
Competitive History

Key: *AA=all-around, BB=balance beam, FX=floor exercise, T=tie, UB=uneven bars, VT=vault*

2012
US Olympic Trials, San Jose, California: 7th–BB
Visa Championships, St. Louis, Missouri: 6th–BB
Secret US Classic, Chicago, Illinois 3rd–BB(T)

2009
Visa Championships, Dallas, Texas: 4th–BB
CoverGirl Classic, Des Moines, Iowa: 2nd–BB

2008
US Olympic Team Trials - Gymnastics, Philadelphia, Pennsylvania: 1st–UB; 2nd–AA, FX(T); 3rd–BB; 5th–VT
Visa Championships, Boston, Massachusetts: 1st–UB, BB; 2nd–AA; 8th–FX
Olympic Games, Beijing, China: 1st–AA; 2nd–Team, UB, BB; 3rd–FX
Tyson American Cup, New York, New York: 1st–AA

Pacific Rim Gymnastics Championships, San Jose, California: 1st-Team, AA, BB; 2nd-UB; 4th-FX(T)

2007

Visa Championships, San Jose, California: 1st-UB; 2nd-BB; 3rd-AA; 12th-FX

World Championships, Stuttgart, Germany: 1st-Team, BB; 2nd-UB; 5th-AA

Pan American Games, Rio de Janeiro, Brazil: 1st-Team; 2nd-UB, BB

2006

Visa Championships, St. Paul, Minnesota: 1st-AA, BB, UB; 7th-FX

US Classic, Kansas City, Kansas: 1st-BB; 4th-AA; 6th-UB; 9th-VT(T), FX

World Championships, Aarhus, Denmark: 2nd-Team, UB

Tyson American Cup, Philadelphia, Pennsylvania: 1st-AA

Pacific Alliance Championships, Honolulu, Hawaii: 1st-Team, AA(T), UB; 2nd-BB

2005

Visa Championships, Indianapolis, Indiana: 1st-AA, UB, BB; 2nd-FX

US Classic, Virginia Beach, Virginia: 1st-AA, UB, BB; 2nd-FX; 4th-VT

World Championships, Melbourne, Australia: 1st-UB, BB; 2nd-AA, FX

USA/SUI, Maggligen, Switzerland: 1st-Team, AA, UB, BB, FX; 2nd-VT

USA/GBR, Lilleshall, Great Britain: 1st-Team, AA, BB, FX(T); 2nd-UB

American Cup, Long Island, New York: 1st-BB(T); 6th-UB

2004

Visa Championships, Nashville, Tennessee: 1st-AA, UB, BB, FX; 4th-VT (Jr. Div.)

American Classic, Ontario, California: 1st-AA, BB, FX, UB (Jr. Div.)

Pacific Alliance Championships, Honolulu, Hawaii: 1st-Team, AA, UB, BB, FX (Jr. Div.)

2003

National Championships, Milwaukee, Wisconsin: 1st-AA, UB, BB, FX (Jr. Div.)

US Classic, San Antonio, Texas: 1st-AA, VT, UB, BB, FX (Jr. Div.)

American Classic, Boston, Massachusetts: 1st-AA, FX; 2nd-UB (Jr. Div.)

Podium Meet, Fairfax, Virginia: 1st-AA, UB, BB, FX (Jr. Div.)

Pan American Games, Santo Domingo, Dominican Republic: 1st-Team, BB; 2nd-AA; 3rd-UB, FX

2002

US Championships, Cleveland, Ohio: 5th-BB, FX (Jr. Div.)

US Classic, Virginia Beach, Virginia: 2nd-BB; 3rd-AA; 4th-FX, UB

Podium Meet, Orlando, Florida: 5th-FX

American Classic, Indianapolis, Indiana: 3rd-FX; 5th-BB

Junior Pan American Championships, Santo Domingo, Dominican Republic: 1st-Team; 2nd-AA, UB, BB

USA/Canada, Houston, Texas: 1st-Team, 2nd-UB, FX; 3rd-AA, BB (Jr. Div.)

USA/Japan Dual Meet, Houston, Texas: 1st-Team, AA, UB, BB, FX

CPSIA information can be obtained
at www.ICGtesting.com
Printed in the USA
LVOW04s1055270816

502113LV00021B/1307/P